YELLAMUNDIE
VOICES & FACES OF FIRST NATIONS PEOPLE IN SYDNEY

MICHELLE McGRATH

Acknowledgement of Country

This book was written on Gadigal land and Guringai land. The contributors have come from all corners of Australia and their land and waters are a most important part of who they are. I acknowledge the importance of this connection, their ancestors who have walked on these lands before them and all First Nations people who call these lands home today.

Sovereignty has never been ceded.
It always was, and always will be, Aboriginal land.

I acknowledge that the telling of these stories has caused pain to some of the contributors and that you, the reader, may too feel sadness when reading them.

Aboriginal and Torres Strait Islander readers are advised that some of these stories may contain the faces and names of people who have passed.

I have made every effort to ensure that the material in this book is correct and delivered in a respectful way by talking with local Elders and community members. My priority has always been to accurately tell the stories of my 30 co-authors and to ensure that the stories reflect their truth.

These words are their words.

If there are breaches of protocol, I apologise.

Yellamundie, what does it mean?

Yarramundi was born in 1760 and was the leader of the Boorooberongal clan of the Dharug Nation. The European settlers called him 'The Chief of the Richmond Tribe'. He was a leader and notable healer of repute. To his people he was a Garadyi, which means 'clever man'.

He was also the holder of knowledge and would pass this down to his people through storytelling.

Yellamundie is now a Dharug word meaning 'storyteller'.

Aunty Julie Clarke Jones, also known as Julie Webb, and her family are direct descendants of Yarramundi. They have kindly given me permission to use this word as the title for this book. I am very grateful for their support.

About the cover artwork

The artist, Garry Purchase, has depicted a meeting place with a person symbol representing a storyteller in the middle. Around it sit people listening.

There are journeys heading in all directions with campsites along each one.

Multiple animal tracks surround the journeys, representing different animal totems and therefore different groups of people.

This book is a place to hear the stories of many different people from different places who have walked different journeys.

Dedication

My first memory of someone standing up for Aboriginal Australians is very clear. It was my Dad.

When he passed away, *The Fatal Shore* was one of the many books on his bedside table.

My Dad was always questioning and learning.

This book is dedicated to Mam, Dad and Jarrod – the confidence givers.

First published in 2022 by Michelle McGrath

© Michelle McGrath 2022
The moral rights of the author have been asserted

All rights reserved. Except as permitted under the *Australian Copyright Act 1968* (for example, a fair dealing for the purposes of study, research, criticism or review), no part of this book may be reproduced, stored in a retrieval system, communicated or transmitted in any form or by any means without prior written permission.

All inquiries should be made to the author.

A catalogue entry for this book is available from the National Library of Australia.

ISBN (paperback): 978-1-922764-30-0
ISBN (hardback): 978-1-922764-62-1

Book production and text design by Publish Central
Cover design by Tess McCabe
Cover artwork by Garry Purchase

CONTENTS

For the reader	1
Uncle Jimmy from Newtown	5
Mark the former Aboriginal Community Liaison Officer	9
Proud Gadigal girl Alyrah	12
Liam, the first Aboriginal person to work at Microsoft	14
Lesley from Far North Queensland	19
Uncle Widdy the fixer	22
Warwick, fellow of good character	26
Auntie Val Linow the survivor	29
Brodee the firefighter	33
Michelle the carer	36
Les the Gamilaraay man	39
Andrea the Torres Strait Island dancer	43
Quinton from La Perouse	46
Selina from the Yuin Nation	49
Beni the city boy	52
Urban artist Blak Douglas	55
Proud Bundjalung Gumbaynggirr Dunghutti woman Lizzy	59
Lavinia the teacher	64
Raylene from Redfern	67
Uncle Max Eulo the world traveller	70

Sovereign First Nation woman Julie Clarke Jones	72
Lua the author	77
Pastor Ray	80
Gayle from Tabulam Mission	83
Shane Phillips the boxer	87
Brendan the rugby player	91
Aunty Beryl, the bread and butter cook	94
Ben the dungeon master	98
Ebony from Wiradjuri country	103
Jezarah from the Bundjalung tribe	108
About the author: Michelle McGrath	111
About the artist: Garry Purchase	113
Thanks	115

For the reader

The world is full of people who claim to be experts on history, politics, life.

That, I am not.

But …

> I know that Aboriginal and Torres Strait Island people lived peacefully on this land for tens of thousands of years.
>
> I know they were sustained by their unique culture, their connection to the land, their songlines and their belief in the Dreaming.
>
> I know there were hundreds of Aboriginal communities across Australia, speaking hundreds of different languages and even more different dialects. I know that most of these languages are now extinct.
>
> I know that Aboriginal people were once considered to be part of Australia's flora and fauna, and that until the 1967 referendum they were not considered citizens.
>
> I know that when England invaded, there were explicit instructions to kill native Australians.
>
> I know there were frontier wars and massacres that resulted in the deaths of many Aboriginal Australians.
>
> I know that Aboriginal people were forbidden to speak their own languages.
>
> I know that the assimilation policy resulted in thousands of children being taken from their families.
>
> I know all of this still causes trauma today.

I am originally from Ireland, a land and people who were also forbidden to speak their own language when England invaded. My country and my people still suffer because of this invasion. This book is my act of reconciliation, written in the words of my thirty co-authors – the Aboriginal and Torres Strait Island people who have graciously contributed their stories and their truth to this book.

I hope that these stories give you an insight into the pain that many of them have felt – and continue to feel – in today's Australia. I hope it will also give you an appreciation of their strength and their beautiful culture.

To learn more ...

Read this

- *Why Weren't We Told?*, Henry Reynolds
- *Dark Emu* and *Young Dark Emu*, Bruce Pascoe
- *The Fatal Shore*, Robert Hughes
- *Growing Up Aboriginal in Australia*, Anita Heiss
- *Who am I? The Diary of Mary Talence*, Anita Heiss
- *The White Girl*, Tony Birch
- *Home*, Larissa Behrendt

Support this

- Reconciliation Australia, www.reconciliation.org.au
- Indigenous Literacy Foundation, www.indigenousliteracyfoundation.org.au

Watch this

- *Rabbit-Proof Fence*, 2002, PG
- *In My Blood it Runs*, 2019, PG
- *Satellite Boy*, 2012, PG

And for all you teachers and educators, there are so many great, easy-to-use resources that will help you bring Aboriginal stories and truth into your classrooms. I have listed some below. Be brave.

Resources for teachers

- Talk to First Nations people in your area. Reach out to your local Aboriginal land council if you need help: www.alc.org.au
- Australian Broadcasting Corporation: www.abc.net.au
- Wingaru – Aboriginal Education: www.wingaru.com.au
- Koori Curriculum: www.kooricurriculum.com
- Reconciliation Australia: www.reconciliation.org.au
- Australians Together: www.australianstogether.org.au

- The Healing Foundation: www.healingfoundation.org.au
- Kinchela Boys Home Aboriginal Corporation: www.kinchelaboyshome.org.au
- Australian Institute of Aboriginal and Torres Strait Islander Studies: www.aiatsis.gov.au

In the words of Uncle Shane Phillips, whose interview you will soon read:

> **Together, we have to take this to the next level. Our culture isn't meant to be just ours – our culture is meant to be all of ours to share. You can belong to these thousands of years as well.**

Michelle McGrath
June 2022

UNCLE JIMMY FROM NEWTOWN

Uncle Jimmy Smith is a Wiradjuri Koori from Erambie Mission, outside Cowra. He grew up in Newtown.

When I was a little boy at school, Newtown was hell on earth. It was a tough school. It was a difficult place in those times, nothing like it is today. There were no trees, and the playground was concrete. It was a really violent place. There were three other Kooris who went to school there and we formed a little gang. But it wasn't a gang of aggression, it was a gang of protection. When we finished school, two of us went into education and the other two went to Long Bay jail. I heard that one of them died there.

The two who went to Long Bay were not bad kids. None of us were bad kids. Today, I feel that teachers bend over backwards to help kids, whereas we had to get by any way we could.

I had a very hard time at school and at home. I ended up living on the streets. One thing is certain: kids don't go to the streets for no reason. Most of it is about safety.

I had an innate goodness. It came from my Father's spirit and it came from the mission I come from: Erambie Mission. It was a real community. Greed and selfishness are diseases of the colonialists – they brought them here. On the mission we never had those diseases.

The things that broke that community were alcohol and nicotine – things that weren't allowed on the mission. The people who drank alcohol had to stay maybe fifty metres away from the mission. But as I grew up they got closer and closer. So the alcohol got closer and closer, and then the poison was on the mission. And it still is. The '67 referendum that made us citizens also made us eligible for welfare. In some ways, welfare was the last thing we needed because it gave us more access to money and therefore alcohol. It became known as 'sit-down money'.

And when the Community Development Employment Projects started, they were always administered by something like a registered training organisation, and always by a white person. They didn't know what was going on at the mission, whereas if it had been administered by the Kooris there might have been better outcomes. But the point is, this is about self-determination, and self-determination works.

Redfern is a good example of self-determination. Redfern is also a great community. The Kooris first came here to look for employment on the railways and in the factories around Redfern, Waterloo and Glebe. It was easy for them to come here because they had relatives here, they had a place to stay. There were thousands of Kooris here then, and now there's only around two thousand. Kooris developed the community to what it was. Like all communities, they have their issues, but there has always been a lot of great things happening in Redfern. All sorts of things happened in the Black Theatre there: they had church services and acting classes. Actor and human rights activist Brian Syron did acting classes there. The Aboriginal Dance Theatre also came out of the Black Theatre.

Redfern had the first Aboriginal medical service, the first land council and the first Aboriginal legal service. And they've gone right across the country, out of this one place. And that is self-determination working: people in the community, working for the betterment of their community, using cultural ways to go about it.

The school curriculum is not made for Koori kids. In the movie *In My Blood It Runs*, the curriculum and the education system have sidelined a young boy and are slowly pushing him out. This steals his self-esteem and he starts to react and to get in trouble with the police. As I'm watching this I'm thinking, *this is the exact thing that happened to me when I was in primary school*. It sidelined me because there is nothing of substance in school for Koori kids. It's colonialism, it's capitalism. The education system has lied to everyone in this country.

Koori kids want to be taught in schools that are run by First Nations teachers, taught in their language. It's not too much to ask.

Uncle Jimmy from Newtown

The real truths are not being taught. They teach that Lieutenant Cook discovered the country. This is such a powerful untruth. In the fourteenth century, Chinese people were down here trading with Kooris off Warrnambool. Then after the invasion, First Nations people built the pastoral industry and the sugarcane industry. We built country towns as slaves, and were exploited for cheap labour. And the colonialists would steal the wages of these people! These truths are not being taught.

But it also comes down to the teaching of teachers. They are not taught the real history; they are taught the colonial version of the history of this country. I've done cultural awareness training for teachers at Sydney Uni and some of them email me and say, 'It was so good to hear you speak. I knew what I had to do as a teacher but I didn't have the courage to do it.'

Teachers, get real! You are in a position of power. Do the right thing and tell the truth. Don't do what everyone else is doing and stick your head in the sand. Have the courage to stand up and ask for cultural awareness training.

MARK THE FORMER ABORIGINAL COMMUNITY LIAISON OFFICER

Mark is from the Yuwaalaraay people of North-East New South Wales. He is the former Aboriginal Community Liaison Officer (ACLO) at Redfern Police. ACLOs originated with the Royal Commission into Aboriginal Deaths in Custody, which ran from 1987 to 1991. Fifty-five ACLOs were appointed around the state in areas where many Aboriginal people live.

I never met my father. He passed away in jail. My mother, I think she's still alive but I never had much to do with her. I was removed from my parents when I was a few months old. As a kid, I didn't understand. I was the middle child and the others weren't removed. That was pretty hard.

When I was fifteen, I went to live with an Aunty. Her mother and my grandmother were sisters. That was a good time in my life. My Aunty taught me about culture, about where family was from, how we were connected. She talked a lot about living on the mission, about the struggle.

All my family lived on Angledool Mission, about ninety kilometres north of Walgett. That mission started around the late 1800s and closed around 1930. They were happy there because it was their tribal place. But then they were moved almost two hundred kilometres away to Brewarrina Mission: trucks came in the night and took them away. They weren't the only ones – lots of Aboriginal people from missions all over New South Wales were moved to Brewarrina Mission when it opened in 1886.

They were always looking over their shoulders, afraid that the welfare people would take them away. One day a kid would be at school, the next day they would be gone. The welfare people would come and take them. Or the welfare people would line them up and take kids off the mission and they'd never see them again. So they were constantly on the run, constantly moving, constantly looking over their shoulders. And not just my family – every Aboriginal family right across Australia.

This disconnection of families, the Stolen Generations, has caused layer upon layer of trauma for Aboriginal people. There have been at least 100,000 children taken from the day of colonisation.

Because of my Aunty, I am connected to my family and my culture. Connection to country means your belonging place, where your family is from – that's your country. Your songlines and all your stories are from there. Going back to country and talking to elders helps a lot. It recharges your batteries every time you go back.

There's a lot of Creation stories around there and the songlines are a part of that. Our songlines go north into Queensland. I know my clan, I know my totems, I know what to eat and what not to eat. My totems are emu and long-necked turtle, so I can't eat them because they're my dinga – my brother. You need to know who you can marry too; that's why it's very important to know who you're related to. Aboriginal people have very strict marriage rules and ways of marrying – you can only marry certain skin groups.

Sometimes other people don't understand Aboriginal people. They want Aboriginal people to be like them but that's not the case. We're never going to be like the mainstream.

Through the assimilation policy, the Stolen Generations, they tried to breed us out, tried to make us fit in. But we're still here, that's the bottom line. They tried to do it for many, many years, and I think it's happened in Indigenous populations in America and Canada too.

Hopefully, as more of our young people are educated, they can be advocates for our people today. That's my hope for young Indigenous kids. There are so many opportunities around for them today, schools like Jarjum. They can help disadvantaged kids to get through that and hopefully get through to secondary school, and then the world is their oyster, they can do what they want. I just hope at the end of the day they are happy and healthy.

Mark, Former Aboriginal Community Liaison Officer at Redfern Police

I hope that the next time you see an Aboriginal person, or see something on the news, that you know what the history of this country is, what's behind this.

PROUD GADIGAL GIRL ALYRAH

Alyrah's dad is Aboriginal. She believes Aboriginal culture is about looking after each other and having each other's backs.

I'm thirteen years old and I'm a proud young Gadigal girl. When I say I'm proud, I mean I'm proud of my culture. I respect it, and also understand what our people have gone through. When the First Fleet arrived people got smallpox and they started dying – parents lost their kids, and kids lost their mums and dads.

I think all children should learn this history so that non-Indigenous people know that we had to put up with a lot: kids stolen from families, slavery, not being allowed to speak our language, smallpox.

People should also learn about all the great things Aboriginal people did. We made spears, we built boats, we invented the boomerang.

My dad is Aboriginal, and I learn my culture from him and my Aunties. That's my mob. 'Mob' is a word Aboriginal people use a lot, and it means we are all like a family. We won't talk about you behind your back. We've got you. We look after the youngsters. It's an Aboriginal thing.

Don't judge a book by its cover. It's what's inside that matters. We're smart – and there's a bit of hurt inside us as well.

Proud Gadigal Girl Alyrah

LIAM, THE FIRST ABORIGINAL PERSON TO WORK AT MICROSOFT

Liam has a successful career in the tech industry. He was the first Aboriginal person to work at Microsoft, and has started a not-for-profit organisation that provides pathways for people in his community to work in the tech industry.

I'm Gumbaynggirr from Northern New South Wales following my dad's line through my grandmother and great-grandmother. On my dad's side my grandfather and great-grandfather descend from the Dunghutti Nation. On my mum's side through my grandfather's lineage, I am a descendant of the Kullilli and Wakka Wakka Nations in Queensland and my grandmother was a South Sea Islander.

It's so important for us Blackfellas to know our lineage. We want to continue to carry the stories and the oral history of our community, and to know who's related to whom. From a cultural perspective, we need to be able to marry the right people. If you marry someone who you're potentially related to, it would not be well received by the community. This tracking of our lineage comes from a traditional practice, but also the desire to hold on to an understanding of the history and culture of each of the families, because of the Stolen Generations.

For me, if somebody's my fourth or fifth cousin, that's my family. In our community, that's what we do and that's why we always talk about our massive and extended families. I've been quite fortunate to come from a family and a community that really enjoys tracking the family history. My great-grandmother left a legacy for my dad. She passed on her knowledge and he

Liam, the first Aboriginal person to work at Microsoft

has recorded it for all of us. When I'm on Gumbaynggirr country at my dad's house we will sit around with relatives and start talking about the family tree and the family history. Then my dad will start pulling out the books and the boxes of photos. And so we're still joining the dots, because we are passionate about finding as much detail as far back as we can. My dad loves that my great-grandmother passed this on to him.

When the first white explorers came through our community it was one of the last points where they had to start tracking through bush to go further north. Some of my ancestors actually took explorers north, and through that journey they documented our language and our words. So while a lot of languages have been lost over time, especially on the south-eastern seaboard, in my community we have our language documented. Up in Nambucca, there's the Muurrbay Language Centre. We've got thick books and we've got dictionaries of our words. We've got northern and southern dialects, and then there's a Nymboida dialect as well. There are nuances in the way words are pronounced. The north and south also have completely different words but they're all still called Gumbaynggirr.

I grew up talking about Indigenous politics, talking about Indigenous community affairs. My dad was inspired by my great-grandmother, who was a huge part of his life in terms of local politics up in Gumbaynggirr. I remember being a young kid and attending the Land Rights March in 1988. It was the first march I had ever been to. It felt amazing – the novelty of being around so many other Blackfellas in Sydney and having my whole family do what would normally only be done on country. I had that whole sense of community and sense of family and I just looked up and looked around me and I thought, 'Oh … I have this network of people that I feel totally comfortable around.' I felt this sense of community and of being protected.

Part of my goal and my journey is to learn how to speak the language. We want to speak it as our first language with future generations.

I was pulled aside at that march and someone asked my mum if they could take a photo of me. I ended up in *Time* magazine. I was just four or five years old, with my red, black and yellow headband. We kept that magazine for a long time. I think it might be sitting in a bag underneath someone's bed now!

When I was younger, even in primary school, I always had the desire to own my own business, and I also wanted to have an impact in the Indigenous community. That was always ingrained in me: connection to community and culture.

But when I started my career in technology, I lost sight of that community connection. Then I had that moment of realisation where I thought, 'Ah, I need to do more. I need to go back to where I'm from and just rediscover myself and what I'm actually trying to achieve.'

I was the first Aboriginal person to work at Microsoft. I thought, 'This is a privilege, and absolutely insane as well because they should have had Aboriginal people before me walking the corridors.' That inspired me to start the journey around establishing Indigitek. I always knew that when I had the opportunity to, I'd start an organisation that actually looks at providing pathways for people in my community to work in companies like Microsoft and work in the tech industry.

Aboriginal and Torres Strait Islander people have been living on the lands for years and creating things that are sustainable and not so impactful on the environment. We were able to create technologies that coexisted with the environment. The physics and engineering behind such inventions as boomerangs and spears have influenced some modern-day technologies too.

Dave Unaipon, who is pictured on the fifty-dollar note, engineered sheep shearing techniques that greatly reduced the amount of time it took to shear a sheep. This technology is still in use today.

At Indigitek, we talk about these stories within our community and outside of our community. Most stories are there to help inspire people in our community to think about ways in which we were inventing and innovating in the past. That's why Indigitek exists, so that people in the community can realise, 'My ancestors were inventors and innovators. Why can't I also be a part of that journey?'

The history of this country is actually 60,000 years of being black, and then 250 years ago that changed. What happened over that 250 years needs to be talked about. Not just the good bits, but the bad and the ugly. It all needs to come out and not be bubble-wrapped so people feel good about themselves and their history. Because what ends up happening is we're hiding the truth, and then people don't understand that a trauma that happened generations ago is still affecting us today. This is just basic human psychology: traumas tend to follow through and flow through families, and that ends up impacting an individual.

Even if they don't realise that a trauma has been passed on from their parents, it's passed on. So that continues to influence behaviour today. To be able to break that pattern, you have to first recognise that trauma.

The truth telling has started. The amazing thing is government is not leading it, society is. The next generation – and corporations – are driving it home. They realise they have an impact and a value. Many young people are thinking, 'Well, historically my ancestors have done these things to these other people. I don't stand for that.'

When I talk about closing the gap, I see that there are two gaps. There is the gap of Indigenous Australia closing the gap towards parity with non-Indigenous Australia in a systemic way. There's also a gap on the other side about people connecting with and understanding Aboriginal history and the impact of colonisation on my community. And when people say, 'Oh, get over it. It happened 250 years ago,' … actually, the trauma continues. And also some of the practices from back then still happen today, just in a modern context.

So, instead of seeking justice, the Indigenous side is expected to lift its game. Well, the non-Indigenous side has to lift its game as well.

Be comfortable with being uncomfortable when learning about the history of Aboriginal and Torres Strait Islander people. Be comfortable with being uncomfortable.

LESLEY FROM FAR NORTH QUEENSLAND

Lesley grew up in Far North Queensland. Her mother is from Mona Mona Mission, Djabugay. Her father was from Wonnarua country in the Hunter Valley. But she has strong ties to Redfern because that's where her dad met most of his family after leaving Kinchela Boys Home, and where he feels most at home. Lesley now works with Kinchela Boys Home Aboriginal Corporation.

My dad was taken from Hugo Street in Redfern as a baby. Redfern is where a lot of the Uncles found their families after they left Kinchela Boys Home. I don't think there's many from the Stolen Generations who didn't go to Redfern to find their family.

I felt that The Block was our mission. It was in the middle of the city and where we all felt safe. I remember dad saying, 'You could always find a bed, get a feed. You were never alone. There was always someone there to yarn with, someone sitting beside a fire. It was a really safe place.'

In winter, you'd see people pulling out their couches and putting them on the fire to keep warm, whatever they could find to make a fire. And everybody would be standing around the fire – people shared everything. And you'd see old people, young people, and all in between, and everybody knew somebody who knew somebody and you could always make a connection somewhere. Didn't matter where you came from.

My father was led to believe that his mother didn't care about him, didn't want anything to do with him. And yet all the

old people tell me that my nan was the most maternal, loving woman they ever met. She reared my first cousin, Big Cousin Brother. And he said she was beautiful, loving. But the documents they have in Kinchela don't tell that story, so lies were told. I get really angry about that.

Dad found his mum when he left Kinchela, and I remember we used to go and see her and he'd say hello, but he'd never call her by her name or call her mum. She was always beautiful and loving.

There's a lot of unanswered questions.

My dad can't talk about these things. I'm nearly sixty and there's never been a right time to have those questions answered. I didn't really know what a family was supposed to be like. I used to think, *this is not right, it was supposed to be like* The Brady Bunch *or* The Waltons, but my family was nothing like that. And then I met the Kinchela Boys Home mob and understood that we all had such similar stories. Meeting all the other Uncles and their children who were in the Stolen Generations, I didn't feel so alone with my story.

I remember the story of dad and the Uncles when I think, *Oh, I can't get through this*, or I'm feeling sorry for myself. I always think of dad and mum, because dad was in an institution and mum was on a mission. I think of that generation – really all our people gone before us – and what they've been through. That really drives me.

We want to make sure everybody has a chance to be heard and let their pain out as we get strength from one another and realise we're all in this together. We can look at the Uncles from Kinchela Boys Home. All they want to do is pass on all their knowledge so that we're strengthened in the next generation and then the next and the next and the next.

They say it takes five generations to heal. That's a long time, but if one generation just does something different and better than the previous, then the next does it better, then even better, even better. And then after five generations, you'll see a change.

And that's what it's about, because we're strong people. We've got to get back to that.

You should not judge people. You don't need to know their stories to be kind to them.

UNCLE WIDDY THE FIXER

James Michael Widdy Welsh is one of the survivors of the Kinchela Boys Home. He and his siblings were taken from his family, and later returned. But things were never the same.

My grandfather didn't want my dad to marry an Aboriginal woman because his other two sons had also married Aboriginal women. And he had the right to stop it because of the law. So mum and dad ran away to a little place called Narromine. But someone told the police where he was, and they came and took him away from us.

There were seven of us kids and we were all taken from Mum when I was eight years old.

My brother Barry was older than me so he had some nights around the campfire with the men. He was ready to go from being under the care of the Mums and the Aunties to being in the care of the Dads and the Uncles and the Pops. I remember dancing around the campfire with Pop and them, and then they'd tell me, 'it's time to go to bed'. I was jealous because Barry didn't have to go to bed.

Sometimes I'd sneak back over to the fire and watch my brother. That was yarning time around the campfire. They would sit around and they would talk. I couldn't always hear what they were talking about. They would draw in the ground and be talking out in their own country, with the beautiful Milky Way and the stars, because there's no light out there. I'd be looking up with them, just looking at the stars. They would throw a stick in the fire and the sparks would come up – it was so beautiful. And they would talk about the flames. How the flames would change colour all the time. I'd be standing there, listening, trying to hear, and no-one would see me. I'd go to bed and think, *I'll ask him tomorrow*. So tomorrow would come, and I'd ask him, 'Barry, Butt, Butt' – that was his nickname, he always had a cigarette butt in his hand – 'what did they tell you, what did Pop say?' But he wasn't allowed to tell me, it was secret, it was Men's Business.

This memory is a beautiful thing to me.

Before that, living on the banks of the Castlereagh River was beautiful. We'd go fishing, yabbying, yam hunting, honey hunting. Our native bees don't sting, so we pinched the honey without being stung! We were loved. It was a beautiful world – until that ride in that bloody train.

I was eight years old when they took us away. I remember we were all at the train station. There was a policeman and a man from welfare. We didn't know where we were going, why we were going. My sisters thought we were just going for a ride on the train. It was an all-night trip from Coonamble to Sydney, and my brother Barry and I showed my sisters the bandaar (kangaroos) and the dhinawan (emus) out the train windows to stop them from crying.

Thirty-six was the number they gave me when we went to that place where we were no longer allowed to use our names – Kinchela Boys Home. At the home we were punished often. Punishment meant different things – floggings, stopping you from having a feed and that type of thing. All nasty things.

Slowly, over time, they put fear in us so that we were too frightened to do anything, too frightened to even talk. They programmed my brain through this punishment and abuse. But the real person inside me, the spiritual person, was different to this. I didn't understand this fight and so I turned to people for help, I turned to alcohol for help. Those walls would come down and I'd be looking for somebody to take my pain out on. When I grew up I had an anger inside. I call it a rage. A flame of real hard fire. But now my tears have turned it into a blue flame, a cooler flame.

I was given back to my mother by a doctor when I was about sixteen. When I went back to meet my people, they formed a ceremonial circle to introduce me to my father. Then they sung out 'widhu' ('white man'), and my father came over and we stepped in a circle. If the police had come along while they were doing that circle they would have punished them because they were doing the ceremonial circle.

At that moment I was shocked, because I had been treated like garbage by the people where I was – white. I wanted to shoot them because of the sexual abuse and flogging and starving to death in that place. And all of a sudden, here's this man and he's a white man – I've got blue eyes – and he wasn't allowed to marry mum because of the law. Then they said to me, 'Michael, you are no longer Michael. You are now Widdy.' Then they said to dad, 'Widhu, you're no longer Widhu. You go back to Jimmy.'

I've got my grandmother's government files, my grandfather's files, my mother's files, and what the government has written about me. There's so many lies in there. But that's all right. When I say it's all right, it's because I have a chance, I'm still alive. But in reading those files I was freed from a lot of hidden trauma that was inside me.

I learned that in 1928 my grandfather was doing what I was doing in 1968, and this is a beautiful thing. We were both into mechanics. I knew how to fix things, and in his report it said they took him from the Pilliga Mission where they mustered up our people and sent them to Barrabadeen Mission to help them fix the liquid motors or the water motors, and there I am, sixty years later, fixing parts of a motor car. Grandfather was also musical, he played the violin and the piano accordion, and today my children and I are musical too.

When you remove a child from his parents, the trauma comes straight away. The child is traumatised and so is the family. The family becomes traumatised in the community, and the community does not understand why this family is like this. They're struggling because someone has taken away their love from them.

And when we go back looking for our parents, we don't fit in. Our community dynamics have changed, our own family dynamics have changed. I watched my brothers and sisters come back and they were different. We loved each other but we didn't speak the same.

In 2017, I was a guest at Government House when the *Aboriginal Languages Act* was passed. That gave me the right to speak and own my own language. People have been coming over here for hundreds of years speaking their own language but we weren't allowed to. Why wouldn't we be angry inside? It's not about blaming or punishing people, we just want to be understood and treated equal. And have a chance.

When I hear words like 'Cook discovered' I think, we were not 'discovered'. We were already here, five hundred different nations. We were multicultural, with all those different languages. I'm of the Warrumbungle mob of the Wayilwan Nation. We were the protectors of the black duck, to make sure it does not become extinct. And we were farmers. We didn't rip the soil or knock the trees down, but we farmed.

And this is our argument with the government today. They said they were sorry in 2008 but in 2017 there have been thousands of children taken away from their families. And still today, we meet with them and talk to them about this and still today they remove the children. They say they want to heal communities but you can't do that while you're taking children away from families.

Uncle Widdy the fixer

I say to the government that if they really want to heal families and communities, instead of taking children from their mothers or fathers, help that mother or father learn how to be a parent, because the love will always be there.

WARWICK, FELLOW OF GOOD CHARACTER

Warwick Yilgari Carberry Bell was born in Balmain and raised in Glenorie. He was adopted and raised by a loving white family, but got to meet his birth mum just before she died.

My mum and dad are white. They are beautiful people. I've got an older brother and sister who are natural to Mum and Dad. Mum always wanted two Aboriginal kids and so she adopted my sister and me when I was a baby. When I was adopted, Mum and Dad wanted me to have an Aboriginal name. 'Yilgari' means 'fellow of good character'. I'm trying to live up to that name!

After the Stolen Generations, there was a stage of forced adoptions where Aboriginal mothers were forced to give up their kids. And I think I'm in that category. I was only a few months old when I was given up. When I got to an age where I could understand it, Mum and Dad explained it to me, and they've always been open and have encouraged me to find my real family. When I was in year 10, my mum suggested I go to an organisation called Link-Up Aboriginal Corporation, which specialises in tracking down Aboriginal families.

My older Aboriginal sister, who was adopted as well, put her name on the list. So Link-Up contacted us both. At first, we just corresponded through letters. Link-Up monitored the whole situation to see how it was going. And then we went a step further and I got to talk to my birth

Warwick, fellow of good character

mum, and eventually I got to meet her. That was within a year. It was special, a special moment.

The first time I met my birth mum eye to eye, there were tears on both sides. She was dying at Royal Prince Alfred Hospital, so I knew I only had limited time with her. I only saw her twice. The first thing my mother said to me was, sorry, for giving me up.

When my mum and dad met her, it was also a very special moment. There were more tears. She thanked them for bringing me up and they thanked her for the privilege.

I found out that my birth mum had four children. Donna, Katrina and Nick have the same father but I have a different father. I was the second eldest. Only Donna and I were adopted out. It's hard to put into words how I feel about that. I'm angry and hurt. I often think how different my life would be if I had been raised by my mother.

She had a rough life. But I'm also just thankful I've got two loving parents and one big family who I am now in contact with.

I learn about Aboriginal culture from my adopted side and from my Aboriginal family. My adopted mother encouraged me to find out more about my culture. She would buy Dreamtime storybooks. And from my natural side, I've got a cousin who can speak Kamilaroi fluently. He wants to teach me, to pass it on. It's always been that way. We pass on the knowledge; that's what keeps the culture alive.

I had a good friend who kept pushing me to paint. 'Try it, try it, you'll never be the same,' she said. So one day I gave it a go – and she was right. Painting helps me to connect with my Aboriginal identity. When I'm painting, it's like I'm part of the painting, I'm one with the painting. When I'm doing my art it's like I go into a trance – everything's blocked out. I'll be there for hours, dot by dot. And when I see that finished product, I feel immense pride.

It's important that Australian kids know the history of what happened to Aboriginal people. Even though we're all a different colour, we all bleed the same.

AUNTIE VAL LINOW THE SURVIVOR

Auntie Val Linow is from the North Coast of New South Wales, from the Yaegl clan of the Bundjalung tribe. Her mother was born on Cabbage Tree Island and her father was from Finland.

When I was two-and-a-half years old I was taken from my home with my two sisters. We were taken to Bomaderry Aboriginal Children's Home. One of my sisters, the baby, died in the home. Then there was only me and Pat. I used to sneak in and visit Pat in her dormitory. They'd throw me into a dark room as punishment. I can remember calling out to Mum and someone called out, 'You haven't got a mum. Stop talking like that. You haven't got a mum.' And so in Bomaderry Children's Home I learned not to mention my mum.

When I was about nine, Sister Barker called me down and said, 'Val, since you're old enough now, you're going to meet your three sisters.' I didn't understand. I thought I only had Pat.

So we were taken to Cootamundra Domestic Training Home for Aboriginal Girls and introduced to Amy, Adelaide and Rita. They were older than me. I then learned that there were nine children in our family. We were all taken on that same day when I was two-and-a-half. Three girls were taken to Cootamundra, three sisters to Bomaderry and the three brothers went up to Kinchela Boys Home. At the time, my father was in the army. While he was fighting for his country, they came and stole his kids.

Auntie Val Linow holding a photo of her and her sister at Cootamundra Girls' Home

I spent my childhood at Cootamundra Girls' Home. Growing up without a mother, it's very hard. The Aboriginal welfare people write terrible things on your files. I was told that my mum was no good. But we know why they took us, because of the colour of our skin. They didn't want black kids hanging around. All I heard from the home was, 'You haven't got a mother. You're unwanted kids. You only got us. And this is where you stay and this is where you live.'

Every day we would get up, do our duties and cleaning. We would walk two miles to school. We felt very alone at school. At the Parents and Citizens meetings, when the other mothers would come in, we would feel broken down and alone.

They were cruel. When we were naughty, they would put us in a storage room. Or they would make us get out of bed in the winter and run around the block in bare feet, in the cold. We got chilblains on our feet! Sometimes they would hit us with the branches of a peppercorn tree.

They tried to educate us not to be lubras. We knew nothing about being Aboriginal. This was an Aboriginal Girls' Home but if you asked the matron, 'What's an Aborigine?', she'd say, 'Oh, never mind, you're educated from it now so don't worry about that.'

We got segregated when we'd go to the pictures. Aboriginal people had to sit away from the white people. And when the girls used to go swimming at the local pool the other kids would call out, 'Here come the Blackies, here come the Blackies.' It was very racist.

When I was about ten, one of the girls came into Cootamundra from the mission. She asked me if I had ever seen my mum. I told her that I didn't even know what my mum looked like. She said if you go out to the peppercorn tree every night and put a cross under the tree, your mum will come. She said to do it at nighttime because God can hear you more at nighttime. So, every night I used to sneak out of the dormitory in my nightie. I would go out the back and get little sticks and put a cross under the peppercorn tree. And another thing they used to say was to put your shoes under the bed and put them in a 'T' and it'll come true, but you have to pray for it. I did that too. Nothing happened. But I still used to go to the peppercorn tree every night and pray to God that my mum would come.

She never did.

But there were some good times too – I had good times with my sister. I had good times with the other girls too. One sister used to go down to the shed and she used to dance a lot. She used to do tap dancing, and we used to do acrobatics and all that and the other girls would join in. Girls used to climb the trees and climb on top of the roof! Those were good times.

When my dad got back from the war, he went AWOL to find his kids. I can remember him coming up to Bomaderry. I remember him arriving in his army coat. And he's calling out, 'Valerie, Valerie!'

I didn't know who it was. He said, 'I'm your daddy, I'm your daddy.' And I just looked at him and the teacher grabbed me. And the next minute, the police arrived and he was dragged away in the police car.

In those days, my Aunty was allowed to come up to Cootamundra Girls' Home to see us because she was white. Aunty used to work in the biscuit factory and she would bring boxes of biscuits for us girls.

But I never saw my mum. My brother showed me a photo of her when I was twenty-one. He told me, 'Don't ever believe what the welfare put on your files. Your mum was a kind-hearted person like any Aborigine. They're very kind-hearted and they're generous people and they help other people out. She'd give the shirt off her back. And your dad was like that too.' So that's the first time I saw what my mum was like.

I'm a survivor. I didn't know what it was to have a mum and dad. Kids today, they're very, very lucky. Very lucky. They've got a home, they've got a mother and father. Us little black kids are still lost, trying to find our way back. We are lost. We're the unlucky ones.

BRODEE THE FIREFIGHTER

Brodee grew up in Wollondilly and now lives in the Wollongong community. She strongly identifies as a Dharawal woman and her grandmother's homeland is Goodooga of the Yuwaalaraay country.

I was always very competitive growing up. I also knew that I wanted to be active in the community. I love and respect my culture and I always enjoyed going to NAIDOC Week events with my nan. I would see the Fire & Rescue stand there and I liked the way they were represented in the community. I knew it would suit me. I joined Fire & Rescue when I was quite young, through the Indigenous Fire & Rescue employment strategy in 2017. I was very eager! Now, four years on, it's a very rewarding job. It's challenging but I love it.

At Fire & Rescue, we work to make sure the organisation is culturally safe. Our community engagement unit has two Aboriginal staff that support this work. I also co-chair the Aboriginal and Torres Strait Islander Advisory Committee. We've been using this network to improve our workplaces and work with communities.

Being a leader is not top of mind, it just sort of happens. You are there for people who don't always get heard, you share the many stories and views you come to hear and hope to make a positive impact. If you have a good role model in your community, kids will look up to that person. If you don't have people to look up to, you could get caught in a cycle of following others and what they are doing. I've seen so many friends not reach their potential, and it's quite upsetting. They missed having a

Brodee the firefighter

role model, and that's what I'm trying to do. To get out there and say, 'You can do whatever you set yourself to. Be healthy, have fun, but do things in moderation.' I think having those people to look up to is so important.

We have a gym at work and I also train on my days off. I've been doing 400-metre hurdles competitively since I was eighteen. I've always been nervous but this is the first year I've thought, 'I've got the confidence. I am good. I can do this.' I love team sports but when I do athletics as an individual sport, when I cross that line first, I'm the winner. If I come last, I'm last and can only put it down to my efforts. What you put in, you will get out. I train every day.

Not many girls break the minute barrier in the 400-metre hurdles but this year I achieved my personal best placing second in Australia in the 2022 Australian Open Championships. I'm so thankful everyone is supportive of my athletics at Fire & Rescue. What I enjoy most is feeling fit, fast and healthy.

Opportunities can come knocking on your door at any time. I always open it, and allow the opportunity through that door. But sometimes that door is locked and you can't get it open. Eventually it will open for you; you've just got to keep trying.

A lot of people have doubted my abilities, and I always tell them 'watch this space'!

It's okay to stand out. It's okay to be different. It's okay to be unique and to have your own voice. Back yourself, and believe in what you are capable of.

MICHELLE THE CARER

Michelle has been living in Redfern since the 1960s, and has seen great change in that time. She cares for two of her grandchildren.

Many Aboriginal people have been taken from their families and put into institutions – some of them horrific. My partner's father was at Kinchela Boys Home. He was very harsh with his own children growing up because that's how he was treated. I think he pushed his own kids away. He encouraged them to work but didn't encourage education to get good jobs. He didn't know how to. He did not know how to relate to his own children. He was impersonal about everything. But it goes back to that institutionalisation he had gone through – he didn't learn how to react to the people around him properly.

I think it becomes almost inherent that you do what your mum and dad did, and they do what their mum and dad before them did. So it becomes almost generational. If the child does not see that someone gets up and goes to work every day, why is the child going to bother doing that? If the child sees that dad goes out and steals, and that's how we live, the child will grow up the same.

And that stems from a lot of earlier families being broken families, with children being removed from their families. If I hadn't been taken away from my family I would have gone to school. My life would have been different. My mum went walkabout and I was taken from my father and his partner. Now it's by choice that I don't get involved with them. I see their troubles, or hear about them. I don't want that. I've got enough problems – I don't want to take on more.

Michelle from Redfern

You need to look beyond what you can see and learn about people. If you want to know things about people you have to ask. If you don't ask questions you don't find out. And that knowledge is power.

I'm fifty-seven years old and for the last six years two of my grandchildren have been in my care because their mother has an addiction and mental health issues. They are lovely kids, they can be angels, but they have had trauma. They have had multiple movements in their family lives.

I look at stories where kids go back and forward to their parents – up to five times, I've heard. My greatest fear – because they have different fathers – is that the paternal families would take them and the boys would be separated and never see each other. And they are close – from the beginning they were always close. So that's the major reason I put my hand up to take them, so they would stay together. I did believe it would be a short-term thing. I know now it's not.

I've lived in Redfern since the 1960s. Over the years, Redfern has changed; women, in particular. They're a lot stronger than they used to be. And there's a big push by women to get educated and to make sure their kids get educated.

Aboriginal women in Redfern have become a lot stronger within themselves, and stronger with their children. They know what they want out of life and they do their best to get it. Before, women didn't have much value, and they didn't have much value in themselves either. There's been a big change.

For my grandchildren, I see that they have the potential to be anything they want to be when they grow up. For me, I gave up my nursing job to look after the kids. I started university and then COVID-19 came along. I'm looking at my options now and may do a drug and alcohol counselling course. And I would love a holiday!

Whoever you meet, view that person as a human being first. Don't judge them by where they come from. Don't judge them by the colour of their skin. Don't judge their clothing. Get to know them and you'll find that they're just the same as you. It took me a lifetime to learn that.

You come to realise that knowledge is power, and if you've got that power you can pass it on to your own kids.

LES THE GAMILARAAY MAN

Les is a Gamilaraay man from Coonabarabran and he works at Redfern Jarjum College as a teacher and Aboriginal Community Liaison Officer.

My biological father and mum split around the time I was born. He got put away, so we moved back home to Coonabarabran, where Mum is from. Then we settled down with her partner – my stepdad – and they had seven more kids. So, there was a lot of us!

Life was pretty good growing up. Big family. We lived out in the country, with a lot of mob that lived out there back in the day. We all played footy together and there were hundreds of us all the time. We never lacked for friends. It was a pretty easy life: go to school, play footy, go to the swimming hole in summer, sit at home in the winter. I really enjoyed growing up in the country. You know everybody, everyone's good to you or has time for you. A lot of good friends, a lot of good mentors coming out of there.

I found my first real mentor when I was fourteen. Funny enough, he was a white cop. I was playing up a bit, out making a ruckus, and he got a hold of me and took me home. I gave him some lip! A few weeks later he got called out to my house and that's when we became friends. He became my mentor. His name was Scott Turner. He's been looking after me ever since.

Then in year 9, I got really close to my English teacher, Mary Dorlan. She was an ex-lawyer turned English teacher, and she really wanted me to get through school. I was playing up a lot and Scott was doing his best, but I needed more support so she come on board. She tutored me, looked after me, and was another good mentor.

And then during university, I was doing some bad stuff and my third mentor came along. Her name was Michelle Brady. She gave me a hand.

I'm very thankful to these people, and I understand that sometimes it really does take a village to raise a child, if they need help or are a bit behind the eight ball. I think the problem is there's not enough people willing to be like Scott and Mary and Michelle. An education is extremely important, but I don't think arithmetic and basic English helps you when there's trouble at home. What's more important at those times, I think, is people to support you.

Not many people are willing to go that far out of their way to support you, to be your person, when they have their own families. Most people would turn it off at a certain time and knock off, but the people who don't, I think, are incredible. Anyone who's down – not just Indigenous people – needs that type of support. But, unfortunately, we don't have too many people who are willing to go that far.

I'm trying to follow in Mary's, Scott's and Michelle's footsteps. I feel like I'm chasing giants but hopefully, one day, I can be a little bit like them.

Mum's been with me my whole life – she's grown with me. She was sixteen when she had me so it was like a kid trying to look after a kid. We're very, very tight, me and my mother. It wasn't always that way, but as I've got older I hit the realisation that compared to what her mother gave her, what she has given me is completely different – especially if you look at what Mum's been given, and what she's created, it's five times better. You can't be anything but grateful.

Because of everything that's happened, Indigenous people just try to stick together. Unfortunately, everyone knows someone battling with addiction. Everyone's got someone in prison. Everyone's got someone

If you want to help, you have to be ready to really be in it, because it's not an easy job. If a kid is a bit naughty in class, it does not mean they're bad. They could just be having a rough time. When done well, being there for a kid can change lives. You can change a life. If it hadn't been for my mentors and my mum I wouldn't be here.

Les with his mentor Scott Turner

dying young. And it's that shared pain and shared experience that leads us to pack in. We are who we are. We stick together.

I think the one thing that has survived the most, through the last 220 years, is a sense of family. It's always been important. You have a child and it belongs to the mob. Most of the time we don't even realise how we're linked to everyone else in our community, whether it be blood ties or just being from the same nation. There is still that sense of belonging between Indigenous people. You're black, I'm black, we are black.

People will let you know very early what you are, and after a while it's become clear to me. I'm Indigenous. I'm a Gamilaraay man.

ANDREA THE TORRES STRAIT ISLAND DANCER

Andrea is a Torres Strait Islander. When she was young, her parents started a dance troupe to share their culture and today she is building on their legacy.

Saibai Island is the closest of the Torres Strait Islands to Papua New Guinea. You can see Papua New Guinea from the coastline in the morning. My parents spent most of their childhood between Saibai Island and Thursday Island, the capital of the Torres Strait Islands. They would travel to Thursday Island for medical needs and resources.

There are over 170 islands in the Torres Strait but only fifteen are inhabited. The islands were named after Captain Luís Vaz de Torres, who accidentally came upon the islands in 1606 on his way to Tahiti. He didn't even put a flag on the islands! No white people settled there.

There are two main island groups: Top Western and Eastern Group. Because of global warming, a lot of our islands are impacted by rising sea levels, especially Saibai Island. It's the flattest island, there are no hills, and it's shrinking.

In the 1940s, we began migration from the islands to the mainlands. The Aboriginal people adopted a lot of our dances and language. You can go all the way to Western Australia and find Aboriginal people who have traces of our creole language, which is like a broken English.

We have so many different influences because we are descended from the Melanesian and Polynesian peoples.

Andrea the Torres Strait Island dancer

We have a little hula dance that we do – the hip movements were brought in from Hawaiians when they came on the ships to our islands.

When my parents got married they came down to Brisbane. It was a journey between two worlds for them. They wanted to keep our culture alive. They thought, *we have seven kids, let's make a dance troupe*. Together with the late Allson Edrick Tabuai, they founded Kiris An Taran Torres Strait Island Dance Troupe. And so my childhood was spent performing dance and teaching culture at festivals and schools around the country. This is how I developed my confidence – I spoke better English than my parents so I was the speaker of the group and taught the dances and songs. I was only thirteen years old at the time.

And today, I am still doing this, keeping that culture alive and educating people about the difference between Aboriginal and Torres Strait peoples.

And I'm on that journey too. I'm discovering the differences between our languages and our stories. And that's what gave me the confidence to venture down to Sydney and join the National Aboriginal Islander Dance Performing Arts School. I always had that vision of teaching and educating everyone about who we are, and most importantly, the next generation of kids. Today, I am building on my parents' legacy.

Our Indigenous kids sometimes find it hard to connect with their identity. They don't always have that solid base with their parents because of all the displacement that has happened. But it's a journey for us, discovering who we are. I mean, we can just google it and speak to people about it, but that's nothing like experiencing going to our homeland and going to different places around Australia.

We're put into this box by the government; we have to go to school to learn this broad-spectrum curriculum where Indigenous culture is always last. When I was in school there was no culture taught. Now there is more, and I have faith in the government that through the school curriculum they will let our culture be known.

It's so important to educate the next generation of Australians about our culture, because they are our future. We need to keep our culture alive.

QUINTON FROM LA PEROUSE

Quinton Silva is from La Perouse. He believes education and sport are very important for building confidence and creating role models.

When I first came to the Redfern Fire Station I was one of the first Aboriginal firefighters, and now about half of the crew are Indigenous.

I come from La Perouse. Over the years, I've seen massive change there – from extreme poverty it's improved massively. We want to continue moving forward. We're very lucky where we are in Sydney: we have access to education and support networks. In country missions and towns, Aboriginal people are away from everything, stuck in that cycle of poverty. Those who have the opportunity will usually leave – they come to places like Redfern, come to the city for work, to make a life for themselves.

My generation is focused on education. I got skills, did the HSC, and came back into the community to work. My work is to help my community. I'm currently on the board of the La Perouse Local Aboriginal Land Council and I'm also chair of the La Perouse Panthers Sporting Aboriginal Corporation.

Sport is so important. Education is number one, but sport is what gets everyone together to have fun. Having sport kept me out of trouble. I wouldn't go out at night because I wanted to be able to perform in footy. I wanted to play professionally – for Aboriginal people, it's a driving force. This comes back to having goals. As a kid growing up, if you don't have any of those goals and you sit around doing nothing, you'll be aimless, following the wrong crowd, being led astray, stuck in that cycle and never getting out of it.

Quinton from La Perouse

We are stereotyped. It happens a lot, it's how outsiders look at us. Most people just don't understand Aboriginal people. They never had an Aboriginal family in the area – all they see or hear is on the news, which is often negative.

Shame seems to be ingrained in Aboriginal people's DNA. It's something you carry from birth. Sometimes, if I see Blackfellas doing something wrong, I sort of feel that it comes back to me personally, but I shouldn't. It's the individual. It's a weird thing. I try to understand it. I don't want my daughters to feel it.

Confidence is the opposite to shame and the next generation has that confidence, whereas a person of my generation often doesn't. I found in our family a lot of strong people to look up to, Uncles and Aunties who have roles in the community.

My biggest role model was my father, because of his work ethic. He was my best friend; it was devastating when we lost him. And now I'm a role model in my community. A lot of my generation look up to me. In rugby league, I want to be the best player, be a leader. I'm thirty-eight and I was captain and now I've transitioned to coach. I still also play for the La Perouse Panthers. I still feel strong but it's a violent sport. I need to retire, and let the body heal.

My father was born and raised in Redfern, and my mother was from La Perouse. There was a big rivalry between the two Aboriginal communities. It's all sorted now, but I'm the child of a Romeo and Juliet story. My father told a lot of stories about dating my mum. There was territorial rivalry, you wouldn't go into this or that area. When we played rugby league against each other it would be vicious, confrontational.

I've been here almost ten years and I've seen the community change massively. The heroin epidemic in the '90s was huge. It affected our families, everyone's family. Crime here was probably the highest in Australia. It was dangerous. But it's nothing like that now. Drugs are still an issue and it's not just an Aboriginal problem. Moving forward, the new generation of Aboriginal kids here will be more positive, more proud and have less shame.

The number one thing I've been taught is family. Look after your family. Be a good role model and your family will get strength from each other. In the Aboriginal community, the whole community is a family. We try to bring each other up.

SELINA FROM THE YUIN NATION

Selina is from the Yuin Nation on the Far South Coast of New South Wales and also Gunaikurnai in Gippsland, Victoria. She lives in La Perouse.

My dad was a fisherman. When he was fourteen, he was given a Certificate of Exemption and sent away from his family and home at Wreck Bay. Because he was fair he was told he could live in the white community and get a job. If he wanted to visit his parents at Wreck Bay, he had to get permission.

We were the only Koori family in Bermagui. I copped racism on both sides. My family would call us 'abbas' ('white') while the non-Indigenous people would call us blacks or coons. I can remember being six years old copping this racism. And when I would go to visit my nan, my cousins would call me names and it hurt. But then you get used to it and you just manage it. You manage to push it away.

Because some of the kids didn't have enough food, they'd come to our house and Mum and Dad would make sure there was plenty of food not only for us kids, but also for everyone on the mission.

When I was fourteen, I decided I wanted to live in Wallaga Lake with my grandparents. I felt like a sense of belonging living there with my nan. That was home. I felt a connection to the earth. I loved just going down to the lake, fishing and sitting there for hours. And sometimes some of us older ones would go down there and fish, and we'd watch the little ones, and sit and talk. Sometimes we'd even take our school bags and do some of our homework down at the river. We'd light the fire, get some oysters and just throw them in the fire. We'd have a feed sitting there

talking and laughing. We got what we call bimbala which are clams, oysters, mussels. My grandparents didn't have to come and sit with us there because they could see us from the back veranda.

As Indigenous people, we have a connection to the earth. You feel it, things that, I suppose, non-Indigenous people don't feel. Sometimes you can be walking, and you just feel, 'Oh, I shouldn't be going that way. I've got to go this way.' It's a connection with the earth and the land.

We knew how much food to take. When we were getting berries while walking to the water we knew we could only take so much. If we were going to pick blackberries, Mum would always say, 'Take a stick, and hit the ground so the snakes feel the vibrations.' This gave the animals time to go and hide. So we grew up learning how to not only look after ourselves but how to protect the animals around us as well.

I call La Perouse 'home away from home'. But it's not like the South Coast. You don't smell the salt water. The bushes smell different. Sometimes when I'm driving back down the coast and we get down past Wollongong and down towards Kiama, I would get the smell of the salt water. And I just think, *Ah, I'm home.*

School should be a safe place for all kids. But some Aboriginal families don't like coming to the school gate. Some parents didn't have a good time at school, some of them can't read or write, and they just refuse to come into the school because of that. They don't feel comfortable.

Teachers and principals need to be educated about Aboriginal culture, Aboriginal connection and kinship. Many Koori kids have lots of Uncles and Aunties. They may call their Aunties 'mum'. Those Aunties will also fill the role of mother. My kids call my sister 'mum' and they know she is there for them. Sometimes, if they need anything, she'll be there before me or they'll talk to her before me. And that doesn't bother me because that's her role as much as mine.

And so this is why you might see Aunties coming to the school instead of the mothers. The role of parents is shared.

Don't be scared to approach a Koori or Torres Strait Island kid. You could end up being their best friend. Be the first in your family to break that barrier down – be open to learning about our culture!

BENI THE CITY BOY

Beni is a mix of several races. His mum was born in the Torres Strait Islands on Thursday Island and lived on Murray Island. He is related to Eddie Mabo. He also has ties to the Butchulla people from Fraser Island.

I was born in Redfern and lived between Redfern and Woolloomooloo as a child.

I'm a city boy. I love surfing and going to the beach. But I also love spending time in the bush. Recently, I spent some time in northern Queensland. I worked with bees and did a carpentry apprenticeship. I've been to Thursday Island and to Murray Island. It is really beautiful and there are lots of sea turtles!

Living in the city is not as simple as living in the bush. It's full on. I gave up my mobile phone because I want to live a more simple life.

I'm a Christian – it's a big part of who I am. In the Torres Strait Islands, there is a celebration called the Coming of the Light. Every year, on the first of July, they celebrate the arrival of Christianity to the islands. Before Christianity arrived, we were into a bit of black magic and cannibalism, but the Gospel brought peace and unity. The people were no longer living in fear – they began to live at peace with others.

When we celebrate the Coming of the Light, each island celebrates with dance. Murray Island has its own dance that celebrates when the Gospel came to the island. That means a lot to me.

I've grown up surrounded by Christian teachings. I went to a Christian school, Saint Ignatius' College Riverview. I got a bursary and I lived there for six years as a boarder. And that's why I worked at

Beni the city boy

Redfern Jarjum College, to practise my Christian values. I'm glad to be where the focus is on the young children. Early intervention works – starting young is important.

I want to work with youth. There's a lot of work that needs to be done. They need good role models. Looking from a Christian perspective, I see that they need love and they need to also feel like they're part of something positive and connected. They need to be given positive goals to reach. Hopefully then they can have a vision they can work towards in their life.

I believe that faith is important, and I think it would be really good for young people to consider that spiritual aspect of having a faith. I want those positive teachings for them.

But I'm glad to be who I am, an Aboriginal and Torres Strait Island person. I hope I can work with Indigenous and non-Indigenous people together to achieve positive outcomes for our people.

Some people might think that Christianity has had some negative impact on Aboriginal people but I really believe it and value it – I know it's been a positive influence in the lives of other Aboriginal people who I know, and definitely Torres Straight Island people. It has been the most positive influence in my life!

URBAN ARTIST BLAK DOUGLAS

Blak Douglas is an urban Aboriginal artist. He won the 2022 Archibald Prize for 'Moby Dickens'.

I was born in Blacktown and raised in Penrith. I grew up watching my Uncles who were famed signwriters. They produced commercial art on all manner of surfaces. For me it began as a hobby but now it is my vocation.

I get asked by high-school students, 'What motivates you?' And I say, 'The rent!' Of course, the inherent thing that motivates me is that it does not look like we are going to have constitutional change within my lifetime.

In high school I encountered racism. It wasn't towards me, it was towards Dad, because the other kids saw that he was black. Almost one in three people in jail are Aboriginal. It's because most Blackfellas retaliate in the way they feel most comfortable and that's to punch someone in the face. And so, when kids would call my dad names I'd just smack 'em and I'd end up in the principal's office. That is the beginning of a cycle that ends up with one in three people in jail being Aboriginal.

> **The boss kicks the white man.**
> **He kicks the black man.**
> **The black man kicks the black woman and the black woman neglects the black kids.**

Kaye Bellear, from *Because A White Man'll Never Do It*, Kevin Gilbert 1973

Schoolkids today should know about the massacres and the slavery, to acknowledge the injustices that were caused. Paul Keating's Redfern speech is a great place to start.

I guess, fundamentally, the thing that is most precious about Aboriginal culture is

Urban artist Blak Douglas

generally the respect and the way the kin interact with each other. And what is most endearing about culture across the board is how we speak with and care for the elders. The turning point for me was, when I was growing up in white suburbia, speckled with other Aboriginal families or people with different ethnicity, I noticed that there was a consistent template for the way respect was delivered among black people. And it seemed to be generally different from white people. And once you've been to a remote community that still has lore, it's further implemented.

But society is so out of joint today, with problems that affect modern-day Aboriginal culture. It's obviously hard to instil that old-school ethic of respect in the average kid who is coming from a very harsh domestic background. But when you have that respect and cultural lore in place, it basically fertilises love. At the end of the day that's what it's all about. That kinship in remote communities, where everyone is looking after each other, has sadly become so diluted – especially because of the Stolen Generations. A very conniving way of dissipating culture.

To quote Warumpi Band in 'Blackfella/Whitefella', 'stand up and be counted'. Get involved in protests. I will continue to paint about the repression and oppression of Aboriginal people within colonisation because there's no such thing as post-colonisation. We're in colonisation now.

Excerpt from Paul Keating's Redfern Park Speech, 10 December 1992

Isn't it reasonable to say that if we can build a prosperous and remarkably harmonious multicultural society in Australia, surely we can find just solutions to the problems which beset the first Australians – the people to whom the most injustice has been done.

And, as I say, the starting point might be to recognise that the problem starts with us non-Aboriginal Australians.

It begins, I think, with that act of recognition.

Recognition that it was we who did the dispossessing.

We took the traditional lands and smashed the traditional way of life.

We brought the diseases. The alcohol.

We committed the murders.

We took the children from their mothers.

We practised discrimination and exclusion.

It was our ignorance and our prejudice.

And our failure to imagine these things being done to us.

With some noble exceptions, we failed to make the most basic human response and enter into their hearts and minds.

We failed to ask – how would I feel if this were done to me?

As a consequence, we failed to see that what we were doing degraded all of us.

If we needed a reminder of this, we received it this year.

The Report of the Royal Commission into Aboriginal Deaths in Custody showed with devastating clarity that the past lives on in inequality, racism and injustice.

In the prejudice and ignorance of non-Aboriginal Australians, and in the demoralisation and desperation, the fractured identity, of so many Aborigines and Torres Strait Islanders.

PROUD BUNDJALUNG GUMBAYNGGIRR DUNGHUTTI WOMAN LIZZY

Lizzy was taken from her mum at three years old. When she was young she did not even know she was Aboriginal. She only found out when she found her birth certificate.

I was around three years old when I was taken from my mum. I remember going in a car and never coming back. I had forty-seven different foster carers and went to forty-seven different primary schools.

School was my haven, believe it or not. Even though I went to so many different schools, it was my haven. I was just shipped from one foster home to another – it made it harder for your family to find you. My mother wasn't exactly a healthy parent back then, but I had healthy grandparents, healthy Aunties, healthy Uncles. But they still weren't allowed to raise me. I remember one time, when I was seven years old, I was forced to eat steak and kidney, and it made me physically sick. I spewed up, and then, because I spewed up the food, they locked me in the shed with the dogs for two days.

It helped when I did well at school. The more awards I got to take home and the more gold stars I got on my little uniform meant I didn't get as badly throttled when I got home.

And I thought, *I've had enough of the neglect and abuse, I've had enough of not being treated properly*. There were some families that weren't like this, that were the nice ones. So when I was in a bad situation, I would be the naughty child to make them send me somewhere else. I knew it was wrong, but I knew that if I did something

Proud Bundjalung Gumbaynggirr Dunghutti woman Lizzy

bad, they'd pack my little suitcase up and they'd take me back to the office. And I'd wait again for someone else to come along, and maybe then someone would tell me that I'm worthy and I'm good and give me some little hope that I'm going to be more than just this black stain on the world.

I didn't even know I was Aboriginal. They didn't even tell me that. They hid it from me. I found my birth certificate in some nun's petty cash safe drawer. I found my little pink piece of paper and it said, 'Father: Aboriginal'. At first, I was really confused and really heartbroken, and didn't know who I was at all. In the foster homes, I had been taught that Aboriginals are savages and thieves and alcoholics and homeless. All those stereotypes.

Now I know I'm a proud Bundjalung Gumbaynggirr Dunghutti woman, from the Mid North Coast of New South Wales. I'm currently living on Gadigal land in Marrickville.

I found my father when I was thirteen. I went home to the mission, to Bowraville. It was the culture shock of all culture shocks. I went from white, pristine, Christian, Catholic foster care to an Aboriginal mission. The mission was scary, but I had all these beautiful family saying, 'Bub, you've finally come home.'

And I found out my dad wasn't a drunk. He used to be the manager of a tea tree farm. He used to have white people as his employees. My Aunties told me that my mum and dad were married but because mum was white and daddy was black, the government had the right to take me.

And that's why I am who I am today. With all the stuff that was done wrong, legally, by this system, it's now my duty, my prerogative, my cultural calling, to try and dismantle all this. Everything.

It's hard to know that when someone sees you all they see is, 'You're black.' I don't teach my children colour until they come

I say to my boys, 'How are you black? You're human. You're spiritually connected to a land that has the oldest continuous living culture known to mankind. You are so much more than black. You are all the colours, you are all the numbers, you are all the stars. You are everything. You are not just the black boy.'

home to me and cry, 'They called me black.' My sons didn't know what black was until someone told them they're black.

First Nation women are born warriors. It's just part of us. We are the matriarchs. So it's part of us to always protect, always nurture, always care, always listen to the land, have faith in our lore, be strong. Community is how we've survived. Otherwise, there would be none of us left. So it's all about community. We are all on the same level.

Everything we do in our culture is through circles: birthing circles, dancing circles, marriage circles, family circles, community circles. You can't find a corner in a circle. You can't find a side. We don't have kings and queens, but our elders are like the kings of the tribe. And the elder will make you feel just as important and as powerful as them. Otherwise they're not the elder they're meant to be.

Underneath Black Lives Matter there is so much more. Black land matters. Black lore matters. Black love matters. Black legacy matters. It's not just about us saying, 'Hey officer, stop killing us.' It's about, 'Everybody help us to dismantle this system that's allowing them to continue to kill us with no accountability.'

Lizzy's poem

When she was young and in the most horrible, darkest times of foster care, Lizzy used to write poetry just to get out of her reality. She still writes today, and has written this for the readers of this book.

> You are everything my ancestors dreamed of because you're the future that's going to stop this.
>
> You're going to be the ones that finally learn to grow and love and live, and align with us in that circle, not in separate boxes.
>
> You're going to come to our circle and watch all our circles keep the ripple effect going, like you have in the ocean.
>
> The wave comes in, the wave goes out. This way we can finally get the wave of whitewash to flow back out.
>
> We can get back to the true aligning, the true meaning of the ocean, of how we're meant to live together.
>
> Back to the ebb and flow of humanity.
>
> Because, right now, what we've got is the pull and tug of racism.

LAVINIA THE TEACHER

Lavinia is a Yuwaalaraay and Gamilaraay woman from North West New South Wales. She is a classroom teacher at Gawura Aboriginal school.

As a young teenager, I faced a lot of the issues impacting my home community. To break the cycle of intergenerational trauma and strengthen opportunities, my parents decided that I would go to school in Sydney. I went to high school one thousand kilometres away from my home town. Disconnected from my community and all I knew, I struggled with this move. My relationship with education has been a rocky one, but I always managed to use it as a tool to pull me through challenges and overcome obstacles.

When I first came down to Sydney I lived with my nan and went to Tempe High School. Struggling with typical teenage issues along with cultural identity and missing home, I was a bit of a handful! Then my sister took me in when I was in year 11 and year 12. The kinship system is still strong in our family and when help is needed, there is always someone there to support. That's the traditional way, everyone has a responsibility. My older sister looked after me as a mum when I lived with her. In our traditional kinship-based system, you didn't have one mother: you had your 'tummy mother', gunii (pronounced *goo. nee*), and all your Aunty mums, walgun (pronounced *wol.gun*). You didn't have one dad: you had your dad and all your Uncle dads. Many Aboriginal families still live with these principles and cultural expectations.

I often think of some of the very first things my parents ever said to me. They placed a lot of emphasis on education as a pathway to be able to have a life that's

Lavinia the teacher

successful, where we can work towards equality, be comfortable in our skin and put ourselves in a position where we can make change for our families and communities and also for the wider education of our country. So it was always one of my dreams to teach and be a person who could create a culturally safe space for Aboriginal students to come and learn, to have academic success and thrive in their cultural identities.

It's been a rocky journey for me but I am grateful for my learning and experiences. I understand the importance of being in a place where I can facilitate that change and also bring my cultural knowledge into the classroom, supporting and guiding students to learn more of culture and be proud of that, belong to that, and how to use it as a positive rather than see it as a disadvantage.

Nova Peris said, 'White Australia has a black history.' And once we start looking at this as a shared history, we're going to start to see the value in our future together. Australia doesn't lose their history, they gain ours.

Our elders say, the healing process comes back down to the most natural path. You admit you've done something wrong, you address the reason why it was done wrong, and you put in practices to be able to resolve those issues so they're never done again. What we're currently facing in Australian society is that these wrongs are continuing to happen.

We all need to be made aware of differences being a positive thing, rather than being a negative thing. We only have to look at the news at the moment and just see some of these protests like Black Lives Matter. There is a need for protest, there is a need for voices, but there's also a need for a place in our classrooms to be able to educate our students in a manner that supports students' understanding in a holistic way.

Cultural beliefs and practices encourage us to believe in something bigger than ourselves. We are designed for a purpose; when we realise that each and every one of us is important and our voices matter, we get to play our part in that bigger purpose.

The sooner everybody understands their journey and their own narrative and the importance of being able to walk that, free of constraint, the better we'll all be able to collaboratively create a story that is reflective of all who walk these Lands.

RAYLENE FROM REDFERN

Raylene grew up without her biological dad. He was in prison the first time she met him. She now works at Redfern Jarjum College and wants to be a role model for young Aboriginal kids.

I grew up in Redfern, with my mum and my stepfather, who were white. They had two more girls later, my sisters. When they separated my mum wanted us three girls to stay together, and so we all lived with my stepfather. To me, I'd only ever known him as my dad. A dad is there when you're sick, he ties your laces. I used to drive sitting on his lap in the car. I was his little girl for several years before the other two came along.

But, from my understanding, my Aboriginal grandmother didn't like the idea of me living in that house without my biological mum. So when I was eight, my biological dad, who was in jail, applied for custody of me and I was taken to live with my nan, who fostered me. I remember when my dad (stepfather) took me there. He said, 'I'll come back and pick you up.' But he never came back. I felt like I'd been ripped from my home, where I felt safe and secure and loved, and I had my siblings and grew up in a family.

Suddenly, I was on my own.

I recall that we went to the jail to see my nan's son, my biological dad. It was just terrifying to be taken to a prison and to be told that this person, behind the glass screen in the prison, is your dad.

Even though I was brown-skinned with my white family, I never saw my colour as being different to them. When I came to my nan I was thrown into Redfern Public School and into dancing with the other Aboriginal kids. At school, I didn't feel accepted by the Aboriginal kids as much. I experienced a lot of bullying. I felt that I was seen as being different, leaving me confused and caught between two worlds. The bullies turned me into a bully for a while. Then I realised that's not who I am. That's not my heart.

I realised it means something to be Aboriginal. And I wanted to know what that is so I could embrace it. I've got a lot to gain from learning from Aboriginal culture. And I just want to soak it all up wherever I can.

Culture wasn't really talked about when I was young. Now I look at other people who have grown up on country, surrounded by their culture, and I am in awe of them. I don't feel confident to speak about my culture, because I feel like it didn't come from my immediate family like that. I am a proud Wiradjuri woman. But it's completely different for me. It's lost. I'm not confident to share my cultural experiences.

My stepdad and sisters moved to Queensland. Every school holidays I would see my sisters. They were very young when I left, and as we got older, the deal was that I wasn't allowed to tell them how we were related. It was difficult because they asked questions and I wanted to tell them the truth. They were everything to me, because I was there through my mum's pregnancies, their births. I'm their sister but I'm brown. But if I told them about how we were related I wouldn't be able to see them again. It was hard. But when you're a little kid, you don't have that confidence to say, 'No, I'm not going to take this.'

I think I'm now the happiest I've ever been, since working at Redfern Jarjum College. Having the opportunity to still learn about my culture, giving me a deeper sense of connection to my identity and community, through my journey.

Aboriginal kids are close to my heart. I see them as my extended family. I want to use the struggles that our people have suffered, and the fury that we feel, as a fire to drive me in a positive direction, instead of having it weigh on me and hold me down. I can be a good role model for these students. I am able to support them through whatever they're going through as I can relate through lived experiences. I can sit there silently, give them a hug and be the someone who does not give up on them.

> Think about if your family went through what we've been through, see it through our eyes. Then, if you can understand that, there should be a place where we can come together.

UNCLE MAX EULO THE WORLD TRAVELLER

Uncle Max is from a little town called Enngonia near Bourke.

I worked on a station out back of Bourke, where the crows fly backwards, bringing sheep in for shearing and bringing cattle in for branding. It was a good job. Today these jobs are done by people on motorbikes.

One morning by the campfire, I read an ad for Alcoholics Anonymous. 'What's that?' I said, and my mate told me, 'That's where you go to get help to get off the drink.' I said, 'I'm gonna go there.' And so I came to Redfern looking for AA. It was 1973.

In Redfern, I got lots of help. Mum Shirl and Father Ted Kennedy always had a spare bed for me. They helped me a lot.

Now I perform smoking ceremonies. Smoking ceremonies are done for purification. Sometimes I do one because there's evil spirits. These ceremonies are done late in the evening, when the spirits are about.

The first smoking ceremony I did was for the Queen, and since then I've performed ceremonies for lots of famous people, like Oprah Winfrey, Prince William and Crown Prince Frederik of Denmark. I've travelled the world, from Paris to New York.

Uncle Max Eulo the world traveller

But I miss my bush tucker. I miss my witchetty grub and my goanna. I'm living in the white world now. Now I have to go to Woolies for my food!

SOVEREIGN FIRST NATION WOMAN
JULIE CLARKE JONES

Julie Clarke Jones, also known as Julie Webb, is a sovereign First Nation saltwater, freshwater Dharug woman. She was heavily influenced by her First Nation grandpa.

I grew up in Mount Druitt, but every Friday afternoon Dad would pick me up and drop me down to my granddad's house in Parramatta, and on Sunday afternoons we'd do dinner with the cousins and everyone would come. School holidays were always with my grandparents. So I was heavily influenced by my First Nation grandpa. He was the one I put on the pedestal: the God, the idol, the everything. He taught me a lot of lessons. I had a big life-altering experience when he passed away when I was eight and a half.

I made a promise to myself that everything I did in my life was going to be to honour my grandpa and my mob. Absolutely everything I do is about honouring him. I guess I'm still that little nine-year-old girl who just wants to make her grandpa proud.

I am deeply embedded in my culture. I deeply believe my culture. It's not *part* of who I am – it *is* who I am.

My mum's generation didn't have the opportunity to do much culturally – it wasn't safe. My Uncle was a fluent language speaker but when he went to school my pop told him, 'Keep it all in here in your head and your heart. Don't let it come out because you'll get taken away.'

I've got this great family who have fought extremely hard to hold onto and maintain every little bit of oral history that we've ever had. And now we are beginning

Sovereign First Nation woman Julie Clarke Jones

to pull that together into a more complete record of our cultural ways and ceremonies and traditions.

We live in a world where white documentation is the only accepted form of validity. That just wasn't our way. We weren't a written people. So it's been a really big combined effort over decades and decades to be asking our elders and our Aunties and Uncles and other mobs, 'What do you remember?'

I was always taught that no one family, or no one person, holds all the knowledge because we don't have dictators in our culture. While there might be families that hold the responsibility for dance, all families will only hold a few dances. Nobody will have all the dance knowledge because nobody can be better than anyone else.

My family holds a couple of stories, but I don't hold all of them because I'm not meant to, because we're not meant to dominate. We're not meant to have all the knowledge. We will tell our mob our stories. But as the kids get older and show us that they're going to be culturally sound people – when we can see they're living by the values of the elders – then they'll get more and more stories, or added layers to stories they already know. When we think they understand themselves, what they can and can't share, then all is revealed.

It is really important, too, that we teach these lessons on country, if we can, so we can actually connect the kids to the country, to where the stories come from. We have as many family and social and mob gatherings as we can, whether they're over weekend camps or whether they're days out on country. We sit and weave and yarn, and while that is happening, lots of things get talked about around the fire.

Getting people together like that and actually sitting and remembering is particularly important for the Dharug mob. We are some of the most fractured from colonisation, and some of the most shamed and some of the most ostracised, and at the same time one of the most written about.

The cultural obligations I was brought up with were that you have a responsibility to your mother, to your country, to the earth and to your father up in the sky. One of the big lessons that my grandpa taught me when I was six years old was that we also have an obligation to every single person that's on our country, no matter where they're from or what they look like, and whether we like them or we don't like them. We still have a responsibility for their cultural and spiritual wellbeing on our country.

The shame came when we couldn't do those things. When we couldn't stop the smallpox, when we couldn't stop the advancement of colonisation, when we didn't win the frontier wars, when we lost Pemulwuy and other great leaders. Those embedded layers of shame just compressed us, and it was a very long time before people could come out and say, 'No, we didn't give up our culture. You made it illegal. We didn't stop talking our language. You made it illegal.'

Our mob has gone through a third wave of colonisation now. We had the initial stages of colonisation, and then we had the forming of Federation and the White Australia Policy, which brought in another wave of colonisation for our people.

Our country is Sydney, over the mountains to Little Hartley and all the way into the city, out to the Hawkesbury and over to Botany Bay. And out to where we share the Campbelltown lands with the Dharawal. Lots of people came here. There was activism in the 1920s and '30s. Then the Stolen Generation started and people came to Sydney to look for their children and their families and they stayed. And we shared.

But it's really political. On Dharug country, we have two land councils. One that looks after the Freshwater Country and one that looks after the Saltwater Country. Neither of those land councils acknowledge Dharug people, our existence, or that this land is still Dharug land. The legislation that sits around land councils is not good for custodians. It waters down any rights custodians have. Native title was never meant to benefit custodians, it was meant to benefit the government. Being a First Nations person in these contemporary times isn't easy, but being a Dharug First Nation person, even on our own country in 2021, is an incredibly traumatic and profoundly complex journey.

For me, trauma is like this light that's working in reverse, that sits somewhere so deep in my soul and my spirit. When that light starts to go warm, I know I'm getting triggered and try to find out, what's this trigger? What part of my life has got this light glowing again? I don't always see that light as a positive thing. I see it as fingers that start reaching out and poking and probing at things that are buried. This light inside, for me, is different because

What my pop taught me in life is that the most important thing is love. Love for your family, love for your people and love for country. Love for country was paramount because that's what fed our soul and fed our spirit, and then all other kinds of love flowed from that.

it normally means someone's attacking my spirit or my identity or challenging or degrading my people or my family.

I wasn't a stolen child, but I've grown up listening to my family who were. Sitting around with Aunties and Uncles who told those stories traumatises me. Watching their pain is a new kind of trauma. I take that and I internalise that. Most First Nation people, to an extent, take those experiences and those pains and internalise them. Because you want to make sure it doesn't happen again. And that's where the activist is born. That's the space I like to be in because I feel like my people have a voice if we're in that space.

There's two really significant things that my pop taught me, one in his life and one in his death.

The thing he taught me in his death was how to really communicate. For a very long time, I was bit of a little recluse. And then I had a vision. I saw him standing at the end of the hallway and smiling, and I guess things changed from there. My grandad used to take his false teeth out and give me a kiss on the cheek with his sloppy mouth – I hated it. The last time I ever sat with him, he actually did that. When I'm really struggling, when I really need his guidance, I feel that kiss!

LUA THE AUTHOR

Lua is a Wiradjuri woman and author of *The Quinnies*. She grew up in Dharug country near Toongabbie.

Growing up, I always knew I was Aboriginal. But my grandmother was part of the Stolen Generation and so was my great-grandmother and they wouldn't talk about it, which made it really hard for me. At school, they would talk about Aboriginal people and I would feel so disconnected from it. It was always discussed in a stereotypical way. They would play clapsticks, play the didg. I remember in music class how disconnected they sounded from what Aboriginal culture is about. And when I said, 'I'm Indigenous,' my music teacher said, 'No, you're not.' I think it took me a while to start to feel confident in being an Aboriginal person because of the way I look. I've always felt that I don't fit into what people consider to be the Aboriginal stereotype.

Growing up I've been able to make decisions for myself in terms of my culture and reaching out and talking to people to make meaningful connections. I have two Dharug elders, Uncle Wes and Uncle Greg, and have a close relationship with them.

My sisters have struggled in life because they weren't offered the same opportunities as me. Neither of them finished year 12. My mum didn't graduate year 12 either. My dad did, but didn't do further studies. So this is all very new for me because I am the first person in my family to go to uni. If I wasn't supported by the GO Foundation I wouldn't be where I am today.

I recently finished HSC and I got the NESA Chairperson's award for highest performing Indigenous student in Aboriginal Studies in New South Wales.

Lua the author

Aboriginal people are very diverse. They don't all live in the bush. They don't all have brown eyes, dark skin and brown hair. We are all different colours of the rainbow. We should respect Indigenous culture because it is the oldest surviving culture in the world.

As part of this subject I did a comparison of two Indigenous communities, the Yarrabah community (which is a largely Aboriginal community near Cairns) and the Oglala Lakota people near South Dakota in America. What stood out to me was the idea of having a treaty. The Oglala people have a treaty, and have gained a lot of self-determination and power from that. To me, it highlights why it's so important that we listen to the Uluru Statement from the Heart and really push for some common ground and universal recognition of past injustices, so we can move forward together as a country. I think part of moving forward is giving some of that power back to Indigenous people.

If you look at the Close the Gap campaign it's obvious that something is not working. Only a handful of the seventeen targets are on track. I think there is a lack of Indigenous voices in that decision-making process and that's why we can't progress.

We can learn a lot from Aboriginal people and Indigenous people all over the world. And I think a lot of the world's current problems need Indigenous voices to be solved. Indigenous people have looked after this continent for 80,000 years and in 200 years we've almost destroyed it! Look at Indigenous fire management practices and how successful they are, and then you think, *why would we not do that?* Why are we doing what's not working? It's like a presumption that white people know better so we're just going to keep doing what we're doing.

It's heartbreaking because Indigenous people have so much to offer this country, in terms of politics, education, climate, management of the Great Barrier Reef, rainforests, national parks, on almost every level.

The Quinnies is my Uncle Wes's favourite Dharug story. It's about Aboriginal fairies that live on the moon. They would come down at night to eat the sap from the stringybark tree and get the honey from the rocks and collect sweet nectar, and then they would go back to the moon. And then one day one of the quinnies got stuck, and in the morning a bunch of Aboriginal men went hunting and they saw the quinnie and they helped him. And when they set the quinnie free, he promised to always leave water for all the animals, women and babies, so that's why we have dew in the morning. And they promised they would always keep our babies happy when they sleep and that's why babies laugh in their sleep.

We've had an oral storytelling tradition for so long but in this current climate we can't maintain an oral storytelling tradition, and that's why we have to start documenting these stories before they die out.

PASTOR RAY

Pastor Ray Minniecon has dedicated his life to supporting the Stolen Generations. He is a founding member of Kinchela Boys Home Aboriginal Corporation and Gawura Aboriginal school in Sydney.

Very often, the solution enforced on our troubled children is to send them to boarding schools. But when we take kids away from their families, we're not growing parents. You must remember that many of the parents were taken too. And so we have a generation of people – now parents – who have had no parental development. Nobody has shown them how to be a good parent.

I say to the government, 'You took them, now you fix them.'

Parents need to be part of the process of healing. I've been working with Stolen Generations in my ministry a lot. Back in the early 1980s, the first group I was working with was over in Western Australia. Just outside of Katanning was the old Carrolup mission. They were still sending kids there in the 1980s.

So in 1980, we transformed it into Marribank Family Centre. We worked with the mums and dads to restore culture and language, offered employment opportunities on the land and supported the parents. This was a good model; it worked. Many of the families we worked with are still together to this day because we knew that particular way of operating is the best way to teach people how to be parents again.

Australian policies of assimilation destroyed not just the families but the culture as well. Destroying Indigenous languages was part of this too. That's why

Gawura – a kindergarten and school for First Nations children – is so important to us. The children there learn their local language, which is Wiradjuri. In the Wiradjuri language, 'gawura' means whale. It is one of the totems of the Sydney area. The children are coming into a place where they know that it's got that kind of local history.

Give us a voice, give us a treaty and give us a truth commission. That's what we've been asking for. It will begin the process of giving us a rightful place within Australia. Right now, I still feel like we're 'terra nullius'.

GAYLE FROM TABULAM MISSION

Gayle and her twin brother were born on the Tabulam Aboriginal Mission in Bundjalung country.

Dale and I were born in the house at Tabulam Mission. And after we were born, they took us into the hospital with Mum. Then three days after we were born, my older brother passed away suddenly.

Dad went up to the hospital, and he found Mum sitting in a room, with no-one there to comfort her. She was just crying and crying because of losing her child. Because of Mum's grief she couldn't even go to the funeral. The hearse had to drive past the hospital because she was so broken.

Mum was in the hospital with Dale and I for a further six weeks and when it came time to take us home, the doctor said, 'Come back tomorrow to get Gayle and Dale.' Mum and Dad went home, and when they came back the next day, we were gone. They were just pulled into a room and told, 'You can't handle these other two babies. Your living standards aren't good enough, there are too many of you sleeping in the house.' My parents were treated like they were nobodies. There was no compassion shown towards their loss, no understanding. Just, 'You live on a dirty mission, and that's why you can't have these kids.' So Dale and I were taken to a foster family.

My foster mum tells the story that she didn't tell my foster dad that she was getting us. He just come home from work, and here were me and Dale in the cot!

We lived with our foster parents in Casino. My foster mum was told, 'These twins, they're not allowed to have any contact with their family.' But she started seeking out our parents to let them know that she had us. She said, 'They've got a mum and dad, and I'm going to let them know that I've got them.'

My parents would have been feeling so hurt about the way they were treated. I think in my foster mum they found someone who really understood.
I remember my foster mum telling me when she first met my mum she could see that she was very broken and had great trauma. She was a really broken person because of the grief of losing a child. Really, she lost three children.

My foster mum always organised for us all to get together on our birthdays. That was good. She kept that connection so we knew who our family was. She would also take us to see our grandmothers, which was lovely. I appreciated that. I got to know my two natural grandmothers.

Sadly, when I was twelve, my foster mum had a car accident and hurt her back. The Department of Community Services (DOCS) just made a decision to put us back with our natural family. They just lifted us out of one world into this other world. That was hard.

As much as I loved getting to know my family, going back was really, really hard. It was a big shock. There was a big family of us in the house. I went from having my own bed to having to share a bed. My parents were worried too – how were they going to feed two extra mouths? Getting to know my mother and siblings was good. But it was hard: they knew me but they didn't know me.

And then, when I was sixteen, I was missing so many days at school my foster sister, from my foster family, said, 'Look, why don't you come and live with me? And I can help you finish school.' And so she helped me to get back on track with school. When she left to live up north she arranged for me to stay in Sydney and get into Kirinari Hostel, a boarding school for Indigenous students all over Australia. Then I finished year 12 at Gymea High School.

Mum died when she was only fifty-four. Dad believed she died of a broken heart. But the beautiful thing is that I feel lucky that I did know who my family are, and my two mums especially formed a really good friendship.

I was lucky to see my family. Some people who are taken don't see their families for years. Some never. It has made me determined just to live a happy, connected life with my family.

One day in the backyard, my natural dad told me the whole story about our brother and how we were taken away. That was around the time the apology happened. Dad just let it all out. Dad said that when Kevin Rudd did the apology it was the first time in thirty-eight years he had a full night's sleep because of what had happened to him and Mum. That is how badly it affected him.

For me that apology was a big thing too. We all went down to Martin Place and watched it on the big screens. I remember it was raining and it felt like a weight off my chest. That's the power of *sorry*.

Dale, my twin brother, worked for a short time in DOCS. Because of what he had gone through, he was on a mission to help other people. But it really took a toll on him emotionally because of his own experience of being separated. He actually ran into the officer who was responsible for removing us from our parents. He was still alive. That was very hard for him.

There is a reparation scheme for the Stolen Generations. It gives compensation to families who were registered with Aboriginal Welfare, who were taken under their care. But it only goes up to 1969, and I was born in 1970.

It's not a beautiful story. But it's so important to share these stories. Kids may know about the Stolen Generations, but they don't know the details. And I think to tell them a story like that, where your mother lost a child, and then three days later, two more children got taken away, is important.

Aboriginal children are still being removed. Sadly, I think it's because of generational trauma. You have hurting children and you have hurting parents.

SHANE PHILLIPS THE BOXER

Shane Phillips is from Redfern, and has connections to the Bundjalung, Wonnarua, Guringai and Yugembeh mobs. His family has been a part of the Redfern community for over four generations. Shane is CEO of Tribal Warrior.

My mum's family were all Stolen Generation. My grandfather had gone to war and then the welfare comes in, takes all the kids. This leaves a family with trauma. People congregate when they've been through stuff together. And when you get lots of those people in the same spot, they end up matching up and they have relationships, and lots of times they pass the trauma down. Imagine if you had a kid who had never been hugged when they're going through something. Their parents just tell them to deal with it because they don't know how to deal with emotions. So, the kid never gets those tools that parents help kids with.

So, they don't know how to deal with it. Sometimes they suppress it with drugs and alcohol, and when that happens, you just perpetuate the problem. When that happens in more than one generation, it gets really entrenched. But you can fix it. Solutions are there, and we've got the tools. We've just never been given the responsibility.

I was full of anger and hatred and resentment. I was part of the whole cycle. I used to say, 'When are they going to fix it? It's their problem. They've got to fix this.' Lots of our old people, I'd hear them say that: 'They stuffed it up. It's their job to fix it.' Then I realised that they're not going to fix it. We can only deal with where we are, our patch of dirt. We have to fix it ourselves. We've got to be responsible for ourselves.

Human beings are an amazing species. All you need is the environment and the people with a narrative that will tell you your worth and help you with the tools that you need. You unpack the stuff, but you don't let it own you. It cannot shackle you or anchor you to one spot, but you can heal and you can grow.

We've got trauma. You've got trauma. We get that. We don't want the trauma to own you. You have to keep moving and then you will grow. You deserve to grow and you have to grow. That's what we want for our people.

There were some old fellas on The Block: Daniel Ariel, Kevin Smith and Kipper Kefo. Daniel owned a boat called the *Tribal Warrior*. They picked some people who were struggling with addiction and set out to train them in the maritime industry. They pushed them hard. I joined them in the second batch of skippers in '99, with my brother.

Fundamental to every human being is needing a sense of worth, a sense of belonging and a purpose. We all must have these. By using the boat and focusing on routine, they shared this sense of purpose. With a routine, amazing things started to happen for those young men. It changed the game.

I wanted this approach to live on when I started the Clean Slate Without Prejudice program in 2009. In this program, the police 'wiped the slate clean' to allow our young kids to take part in a boxing program that would give them routine, discipline and hard work. The police and the kids boxed together and developed a mutual respect.

Today, I see a lot of families make that change. It's pretty cool, because there's a whole movement of people now trying to drive strength-based communities. You can feel it in Redfern. It has become a place of can-do. I just feel blessed and grateful that I'm part of that.

Mum and Dad were always talking about our strengths. Every day, I'd hear all these amazing things about our people. Before colonisation, people lived for longer. We had our languages in place. Our laws were in place. Everyone had food and you didn't have to buy it: you had to work to protect the land so that everyone could eat from that. We had a really good system – an ecosystem – that was based on this circular way of doing stuff.

We had medicines that helped our people. We didn't have sugars, so we weren't dying of dietary diseases.

We had the stars. We now know about navigation through the stars and about those songlines and how important they are in navigation. We traded – and we did it well – for thousands of years. We had really good, strong family lines and family links. We had things that were really important. It worked.

Our hope is that this information does not get lost. We say to our kids:

Shane Phillips the boxer

'Just imagine that every thousand years, our people had to overcome something dramatic, something big. It could have been an earthquake, a meteor, illness that could have nearly wiped our people out. Our people had to rebuild. Kids, families – they became the ones responsible for taking it through the next thousand years. And now it's our turn. We have to be responsible for keeping this language, keeping all these practices. Let's rebuild them again, now, for the next thousand years.'

Keep an open heart. Learn some of our strengths. Don't tread on eggshells, get in there and meet people. Together, we have to take this to the next level. Our culture isn't meant to be just ours – our culture is meant to be all of ours to share. You can belong to these thousands of years as well.

BRENDAN THE RUGBY PLAYER

Brendan fulfilled his dreams of playing rugby, travelling the world and owning a company. But he believes his biggest achievement is overcoming addiction.

I grew up on The Block. We had different mobs from all over New South Wales living there – they came from Walgett, Kempsey, Grafton. We'd come as one family. We shared and cared for each other on The Block.

We played footy on the street. We didn't have any grass so we just played on the road. We played cricket, stopping the game and moving onto the footpath when the cars came through. Then we'd go to the Tony Mundine gym. There we'd see the elders like Uncle Dick Blair. It was inspirational. Superstars would visit the gym: Michael Jackson, Whoopi Goldberg, Jean-Claude Van Damme, Ice Cube, Run DMC. They came to see the community, to see what it was like.

The Block is gone now. Families lived there, grew up there, made a life there. They've destroyed that. But we have got to move with the times, we can't live in the past. But sometimes the past is what makes you who you are today. People will say, 'It's not The Block anymore,' but I will always call it The Block. It gave me strength. It's home.

Growing up, I had a dream to play rugby and travel. And I did it. I played rugby for Australia, I played for the New South Wales Waratahs and represented my country playing rugby union. I travelled the world, I played rugby in Italy for Benetton Treviso. I bought a house, I own a construction company. I had all my dreams – but I didn't have *me*. Along the way, I lost my identity.

My addiction was the problem, and I knew that the only person who could fix it was me. And so I fixed it. I put myself into rehab for three months. That's probably the best achievement in my life, admitting to something and then owning it.

And now I'm just trying to pass this knowledge on to the younger generation around this community. You do get knocked, but you also can get back up. There's always a right and always a wrong. There's a yes and there's a no. There's choices in life. You've got to make your own footprints. Don't step into no-one else's.

I see Indigenous people as being like turtles. The turtle has a shell, and it's always protecting. The head only comes out when it knows people, when it knows family, when it knows mob. If it doesn't know him, he'll hide in the shell. We have got to break through that. I don't care who's around us, we've got to break that shell and put our head out all the time and be proud of who we are.

Just believe in where you come from. But most of all believe in who you are. Because you might not look Aboriginal, you might have fair skin, but you know on the inside, in your heart, that you're Aboriginal. Know who you are.

Brendan the rugby player

AUNTY BERYL, THE BREAD AND BUTTER COOK

Aunty Beryl is a Gamilaroi lady from Walgett, New South Wales. She runs a catering business and is known for her cooking skills.

Everybody calls me Aunty Beryl.

I'm a Gamilaroi lady from Walgett, New South Wales. I came to Sydney when I was sixteen years old, and I've lived in and around Redfern for the past fifty years. I've seen all the changes – from when we had no rights, to today. I've been with the bad times and I've been with the good times, and I think now is the time for us.

I've always focused on education. To me, education is the key because that's what my elders – I called them my oldies! – always said: 'Get employment and get an education', and that's what I've done. My focus was to take the education back to the community, which I have done over the past fifty-odd years.

I taught my children from the Little Golden Books because that's all we had back then. And they've gone on to have a very good education and they're all professional people now, and I can see my grandchildren have had opportunities to do the same thing because their parents have been educated. And my great-grandies will have the same opportunity.

I learned how to read off an IXL jam tin! I learned the ABC back to front. My kids think it's a big joke, but it's true!

My mum passed away when I was twelve. There were nine of us kids. My Aunt, even though she had eight children of her own, took us in so that we were kept together. She didn't want us to be taken away. She would have nothing to do with the welfare people. So there were seventeen of us in the one house! And we all learned to do our chores. We grew up in a happy and loving, caring family with my dad and my Uncle and my Aunt.

And we grew up with love and respect and caring and sharing from one another because that's who we are. That's Aboriginal people. That's how it is in every family regardless of what the situation is. We were all taught to go out and work and to go off and get an education, and that's what we did.

My elders taught me about food, and we all came to the table to have our meal together every day. There was no TV then. But even after we got television, we were never allowed to sit there in front of it eating our dinner. We always came together at the table.

Our time out was spent playing sport in the fresh air, and going fishing and catching fish for dinner. For us, everything was done on the river. We washed our clothes in the river, we fished on the river, we cooked there on an open fire, and I can still do that today. I haven't lost that skill.

We would cook johnnycakes. My Aunt taught us all how to cook that. And then we had lots of fish. We had lots of stews. And my dad and my Uncle worked for the farmers, so we had plenty of meat and fresh veggies. They didn't get paid much, but we got fed. And because there was seventeen of us, we learned about portion control!

My Aunt taught us how to make bread-and-butter pudding and it was my job to make it on a Sunday.

Our culture is so important, but for a while our mob forgot all about our culture. I can see now, though, that that's all coming back because this generation is being educated. At one stage in the community, the youth had lost respect for their elders. That was really not right in my eyes because that's not the way our culture operates. It never has been and it never will be.

Culture was lost because nobody talked about it. And families who had lost connection to their culture didn't talk about it. It was different with me because that was instilled at home. And if you don't have that instilled in you at home, then you lose it.

But I can slowly see that the young people are coming back into the community. They are standing up and being counted. Young people are starting to bring back that respect and learning their culture.

I always remembered what my oldies said to me – 'get an education'. I'm self-educated and I have a couple of degrees. I've been teaching hospitality and catering in Sydney for twenty-five years.

For years we trained our students and people in hospitality, young and old, but there was nowhere for them to get employment. So I set up my own catering company – it's called Yaama Dhiyaan, which means 'Hello, family and friends' in my language. And then it all continued from there. I became the employer as well as the trainer.

My company wasn't there to make money, it was there to employ our kids and to create partnerships with the corporate world, and I've been able to do that. Now some of those

Aunty Beryl, the bread and butter cook

kids have grown up and they've got a better quality of life and they've gone on their own journey.

Me and my husband used to go on roadies and camping holidays, real camping with just a tent and a fire! I could see that each state and territory in Australia has different areas where different things grow. And then I became very passionate about native food and ingredients.

I like the bush tomatoes; they grow in sandy soil in South Australia and Western Australia. There are many farms on the North Coast where the finger limes grow. In New South Wales we have the honeybee, but in the Northern Territory we have the honey ants. They live under the roots of the trees – you've got to dig to find them and then you bite the back of the ant to get the honey! It's so good!

You can find lilly pillies in Sydney, and the Illawarra plum grows down the South Coast. But I love the lemon myrtle, and my lemon myrtle biscuits are famous! Chefs are experimenting with these ingredients more and more. It's very exciting!

I'm my own brand now. I've done very little advertising, just me being honest and respectful and understanding and listening to people. You've got to listen. And when you do anything with your heart and soul, it just comes out automatically.

This place, it's community to me. I was on The Block since I was sixteen years old, and I've seen all the changes. I've lived through the past, when we marched for our rights and did what we had to do. And now our young people have got to do this. They've come back to The Block and we'll start all over again. They're educated, and so they'll fight the fight and do what we need to do.

If you have an education, you have a voice, you have a choice. And you can stand up and talk on their terms. That's my thing. You do it with respect.

We are a multicultural Australia. And that's the bottom line. And we have to respect that. And the most important thing is you communicate and then you listen. Because everybody's different, no matter what background you come from.

Australians are learning more about Aboriginal people. It's a slow journey, a very slow journey, but we're getting there. It's happening in my lifetime, but it'll get better in my children's lifetime and my grandchildren and my great-grandchildren. They will still be fighting the fight.

BEN THE DUNGEON MASTER

Ben is a gamer and is CEO at Indigitek.

My background is Wiradjuri – that's where my mum's from, over the other side of the Blue Mountains.

When I was young we moved around a lot because my dad worked in the coal mines and studied. But when I was twelve years old we came to Sydney, lived in Redfern, and I went to school in Glebe.

I always loved computers, from when I was a little boy. Back then I wanted to be a robotic scientist, and *Transformers* was my favourite cartoon. My mum would let me stay up late at night and watch *Star Trek* with her, and that's where I got my love for science fantasy from. It was always my mum who encouraged me to play on computers and do computer work.

In primary school at Armidale, we were very fortunate. We had a huge number of Indigenous kids at that school and we had this great teacher – his name was Mr Nolsworthy. I remember him. It's amazing the impact a great teacher can have on you. He introduced computers to the classroom, and so if you did a good job, you were able to go work on the computers, and that's where I started programming. He taught me how to program Logo, which is still around now, and I loved it!

In my first year of high school I had glandular fever and so I missed out on six months of school. I had always been very good at the academic side of school, and always got really good results, so it was a little bit different to come into high school having missed so much and realise, 'I don't know how to do a fraction. No-one's taught me.' And I really struggled with English. I thought I wrote great pieces of work. Students laughed at my jokes in my work. They would laugh and nod their heads, but the teacher just didn't like it, and I always got bad results. But computers are logical. Computers are yes or no. It's binary, it's ones

Ben the dungeon master

and zeros. It's either right or it's wrong, and so I always did well at computers.

Being a Blackfulla who loved Dungeons & Dragons back in the '80s, I was super-nerdy and kids would make fun of me. But I thought, *You know what? I can just be nerdy on the side by myself.*

I was also good at sport, and sport brought Blackfullas together. When you're good at sport you get celebrated. That still exists, that notion that Indigenous kids' only opportunity is through sport. But we should be getting away from that, because that's not setting kids up for a good future.

There is such a stereotype on Blackfullas that sport is the only way to keep them engaged, and it's not true. There are so many systems and disadvantages put upon us, and oppression, that cause us to be where we are. We're still behind. Imagine if you didn't have the internet at home? Imagine if you had one mobile phone to share among three families? You couldn't just have the phone whenever you wanted. There's a real disadvantage there still.

There's also a system in place to keep Indigenous kids from reaching their dreams. A careers advisor might say, 'Well, you've missed thirty days this year, so how are you going to have a job in tech?', when that child maybe missed thirty days because they had to look after their mum.

So when we look at all of these different systems of oppression – things like taking family away, not being able to know who your family are, the whole history – we have to work harder to get rid of those barriers and move forward. And one of the really, really great ways to do that is through technology. I've seen kids from a place called Wangkatha country, where they've never been on a plane, they've never seen an escalator, and they come to Sydney to be part of a Hackathon that Indigitek supported. I've seen them put virtual reality (VR) headsets on for the first time and run around and just be buzzing. They're just like any other kid. Put technology in front of them, and give them an opportunity and access and skills and knowledge, and they will love it – just like anyone else.

This is what we do at Indigitek. We give these kids access and opportunity, keep them engaged, and have them follow their dreams the whole way, like I did. When I was a kid, I wanted to be a robotic scientist. I sucked at English and I didn't do very well at maths, and I didn't apply myself in high school, but I got that encouragement throughout, and that helped shape my career. It helped shape where I am now. How can we do that and keep that going for other Indigenous kids? And then we work with the industry to make it easier for these people to get into careers, and stay in those careers.

There's only a few hundred Indigenous people in technology right now in the whole country, and it's lonely. I was the only Indigenous person in my organisation for 20 years, and the stuff I saw and heard was terrible. There was racism. Being a light skin Blackfulla, people just spurt racist stuff because they think that I'm just another Whitefella at the table and it's okay.

I developed a reputation at my old work for standing up against colleagues and even customers who were making racist comments. Initially I was scared, because I was very young and I didn't know how to handle it. *Do I say something? Do I not? Do I have the support of my team? Do I have the support of my manager? I certainly don't have the support of other Indigenous people, because there are no other Indigenous people here.*

That's how Indigitek came about, because five of us who were friends thought, *we're the only Indigenous people in our organisations and we're seeing some pretty bad stuff happening. Let's come together and build a community, so we continue to grow.*

If you want to be an Instagram tech wizard or an Instagram business or an entrepreneur, you want to help your community, you want to do VR, augmented reality ... all of these things, if you love that stuff, then let's nurture it all the way, and then you can have a career in that when you get older, and you can have social impact if you want, or you can have global impact if you want.

By 2026, over 75% of jobs will be digital! There are so many ways to influence that industry.

I think the most important thing is, if you are interested in technology, if you're interested in gaming, if you're interested in art, if you're interested in science, if you're interested in maths and engineering, absolutely, follow that dream. Don't let anyone tell you can't do that because that's absolute rubbish. There are so many amazing Blackfullas out there who are working in that STEM space. I feel very privileged to know so many of them.

But keep that passion and dream alive because it's incredibly fun to be a part of this industry. There's so much great gaming right now. Gaming has exploded in the last few years, in lots of different ways. In 2021, the number of hours playing computer games surpassed the number of hours watched on television for the first time ever in Australia and New Zealand. The gaming industry is bigger than TV!

At Indigitek we have an all-Indigenous Dungeons & Dragons game. It goes live on Twitch every month. I'm the Dungeon Master, or the Game Master, so I help players through the story. It's only the second all-Indigenous Dungeons & Dragons show that I'm aware of. The other one is the NDND crew from America, which is all Native.

It is really, really fun. I've played multiple Dungeons & Dragons games and they're all different, but none of them come close to playing in a group full of Blackfullas.

It's the same feeling when you walk into a room full of Blackfullas. It's the same feeling when you walk into an Indigitek event, where you see all these amazing Indigenous people in STEM. There's something about being around Indigenous people and being around mob and being around your friends that are Blackfullas. There's a different level of warmth and enjoyment to it.

I was playing World of Warcraft in 2006 and I met this fella, we were helping each other do a quest together because it was difficult. Somehow we figured out that he was a Blackfulla from Gunnedah and I was a Blackfulla from Sydney – I'd never, ever met another Blackfulla playing a computer game. And we are still best of friends.

But sometimes gaming is not a safe place. There are terrible things that go on and men have to do better, boys have to do better. Just because you're playing a game, just because you're hidden behind an avatar, doesn't mean that you can be disrespectful. You should respect people as if they were sitting next to you in class or in your home. I think anonymity, and this lack of physical presence with people that you're talking to, gives some young people this confidence to be sexist, to be racist and to be toxic. If you wouldn't say it to your mum, don't say it.

You also need to learn to think critically at a very young age. Stop believing everything you read online. Not everything is giga, not everyone is a gigachad.

EBONY FROM WIRADJURI COUNTRY

Ebony is from Wiradjuri country in Griffith, New South Wales. She had lots of difficulties at school, but overcame them and is now at university, training to be a teacher.

I was born three months premature, so I was really, really sick, and spent a lot of time in Canberra hospital, and then went to Griffith where I lived with my nan at Three Ways Reserve.

When I was four I fell over at a running carnival. When I came home my mum couldn't take my school boot off. And then when they finally got it off, my ankle was rock solid. After a few weeks the swelling went down, and disappeared. And then one day I was just standing in the doorway. I can remember it, watching my mum change my younger sister's nappy. And I took one step and then I couldn't move, I just remember freezing and holding the door, and then my older sister coming in and picking me up to try and help me, move me. And I just started screaming.

I remember being in the back of the Westpac Rescue Helicopter, on the tarmac at the airport. Nan and Mum weren't allowed to fly with me because there was no room. And they were waving and crying when the doors closed. I was just a little four year old.

The doctors were going to amputate my leg. I got double pneumonia and nearly died. I spent months in and out of hospital.

Houses on the mission were really, really old and prone to flooding. So the wood was like sick wood. It was really damaged. And I got an infection from that, from being in that house. And it was so crazy because maybe eight years later, the family that was still living in that house, one of their kids got the same thing.

I remember very little of that time but can recall celebrating another little girl's birthday in the hospital. Her name was Isabella – she was five. And I can remember going home on the train with Mum.

Growing up, I had a lot of anger. In year 7 I was suspended from school twenty-one times! It got worse when my younger siblings came to school too, because they were bullied. I always prided myself on being kind to other people, especially people who had disabilities or people who weren't as socially apt or aware. That was just me, I would stick up for those people if other people were bullying them. My cousin had a lot of learning difficulties, and other kids would get her to dance in front of everyone in the middle of the school with earphones that were plugged into an empty juice box, and put her on show like that. That made me livid. I would get so mad.

So, that was what year 7 was like for me. I was always that angry little kid. When all the other kids would be playing outside, I'd be sitting in my room, reading a book or doing my homework, because I was so young and dealing with so much. I would sit and watch news stories. And when all the kids were knocking on the window – 'Come out and play' – I would say, 'No, I don't want to. I'm going to watch the news'. I felt old in the head.

I really hated being at home. I loved being at school.

Other things happened to me, bad things. And when the bad things happened, my nan protected me. When I told her about these things she simply asked, 'Are you sure?' When I said yes, that was enough for her. From then on she helped me. I trusted her. I needed to have that one person I could trust. I did not want to become a statistic. Even from when I was really, really young, I thought, no, this is not going to happen. This is not going to continue to happen. I also was driven because I had younger female siblings. I didn't want things to happen to them. Younger cousins also looked up to me. I wanted to pay it forward for my nana. Everything I did from that moment was for her.

My family has a long line of women who have been dealt a hard hand. I have always been aware of their strength. It wasn't hard for me to be the one to make that call to be really outspoken.

Aunty Coral's daughter was taken from her. She was very fair so she was taken and sent to a home for Aboriginal girls in Bendigo, called The Convent of the Good Shepherd. She tells the story that almost every night on weekends, she would go to the window and the nuns would usher her away from the window. But she was drawn to the window because, almost like clockwork, there was this lady who would turn up to the gate and wave and cry.

Ebony from Wiradjuri country

And it was her mum. Aunty Coral would hitchhike from Shepparton to the home. She would stand at the gate to let her daughter know that she was alive. Because the nuns were telling her that her mum died. They said, 'She couldn't look after you and she died, so that's why you are here.'

I was too young to know Aunty Coral. She died when I was a newborn, and yet I have this clear memory of her. I remember the blue coat that she was wearing, the way her hair was, her slippers, her socks, everything. I remember her going out and screaming at the kids, 'Stop running around the pool,' and lighting up a cigarette. And it just makes me feel strength from her. My nan is named after her, and is the spitting image of her. Aunty Coral taught Nan a lot of her values in life and she was the one who Nan always looked up to. It just amazes me that from just that one woman, values of family and strength were passed down through our family.

I pay homage to these strong women in my family. It's not just the last two or three generations. It's that relationship and connection for hundreds of thousands of years. That's what is instilled in us. That's where it stems from. That's spirit. Carried by spirit, spirit of connection, spirit of belonging. When you have a good grip on that kind of stuff, you're unstoppable. Because you know where you are, you know who you are, you know where you stand in the world and you know what you're capable of.

I moved to Sydney to finish high school but problems followed me and I continued to have a hard time. In year 12, just before my HSC, I got suspended again. I went home for four weeks straight. I started to

To teachers I say, take your time to make connections, to get to know your kids more than just why they're getting low marks. Talk to them, have a laugh with them. Show them that it's okay to be vulnerable. Because that is what's going to earn their trust. There's nothing better than teachers who can put their ego aside and admit that they were wrong.

have nightmares. It was the same recurring nightmare: I didn't graduate and didn't receive my HSC and couldn't go to uni. I would have the same dream over and over. I was waking up in sweats, crying. It really scared me. It scared me so much that I pushed and pushed and got back into school.

And the first thing the teachers did, they all cried, apologising. 'We're sorry,' the Principal said to me. 'I didn't even know you. I didn't know your story. I didn't know what was happening. And I kicked you out. I did the wrong thing.'

I did my HSC. I was never so happy to put my name on a piece of paper! I didn't want to have those nightmares again.

I'm so happy that it was me who went through all of this and that I could come out the other side, to use the pain as fuel instead of having that as a catalyst for why I'm not succeeding in life. Other Aboriginal kids might not be so resilient. And now I'm at university, training to be a teacher.

JEZARAH FROM THE BUNDJALUNG TRIBE

Jezarah is from the Bundjalung tribe, and she was taken away from her mum and dad when she was four.

Redfern is a great place. We used to have The Block here. My mum grew up on The Block and told me that it was a place where all the Aboriginal people used to meet each other. It was a happy place.

When I was four, me and my brothers were taken away from my mum and dad. It was a bad thing – but it was a good thing too. We got more care from the foster families. They would buy us the clothes we needed and uniforms and shoes. I had different foster families, but most of my foster families were my Aunties and Uncles. They looked after me until my mum and dad were ready to have me back.

I went to a really posh school where I had to wear a skirt and a blazer. We had to have our hair up tight with gel – my head would hurt!

I came back to live with my mum and dad when I was ten. It was good to be back but it was hard starting in a new school. But going to Redfern Jarjum College was good because I got to learn about my culture.

I have connections to Bennelong and Pemulwuy, who lived in the Sydney region before Europeans came. Bennelong was the first Aboriginal man to visit Europe and return. From Captain Cook Bennelong learned how to drink alcohol and smoke. He had a wife named Barangaroo.

If people don't know much about Aboriginal culture, I would like them to come to one of our Aboriginal people and

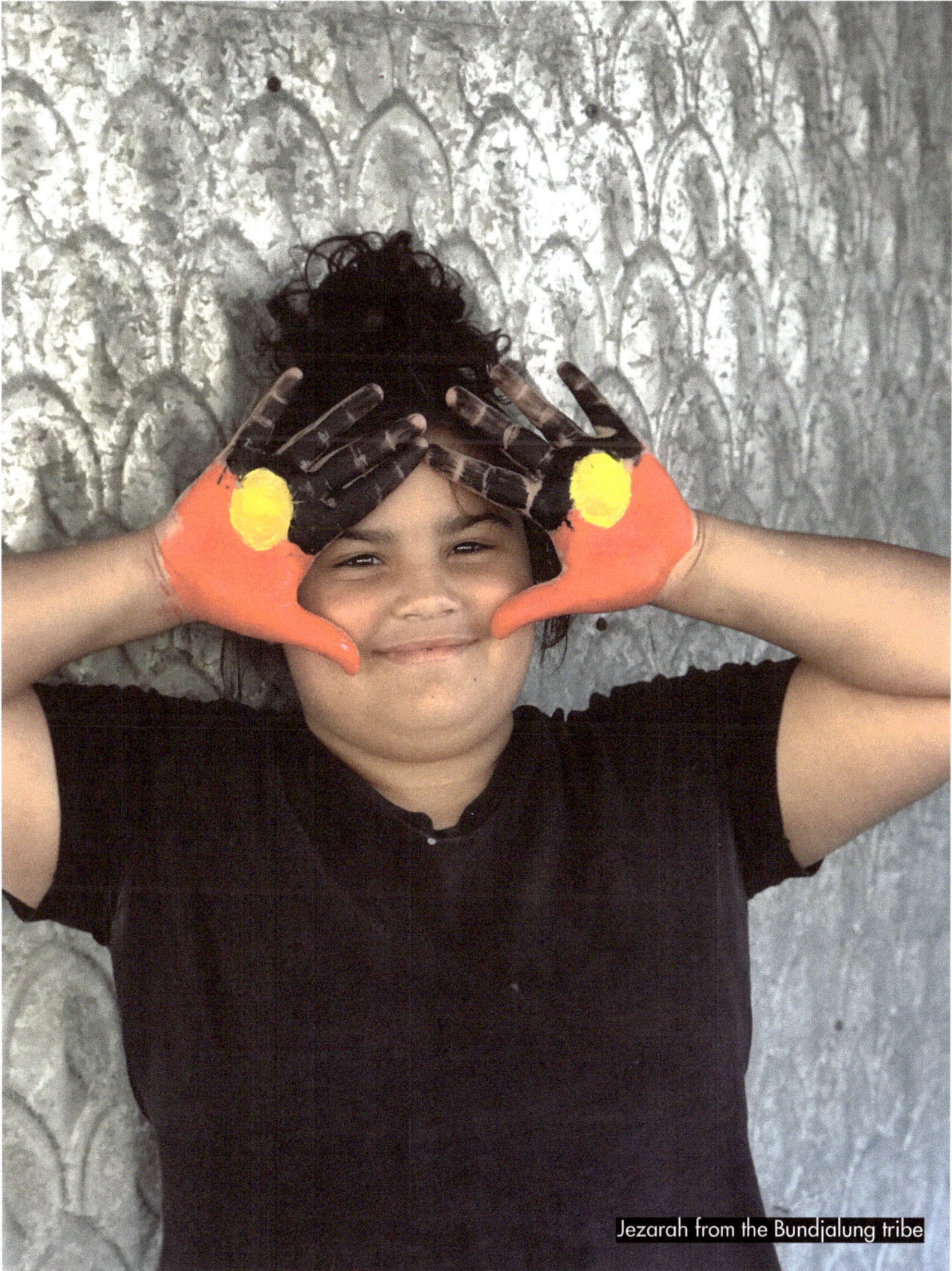

Jezarah from the Bundjalung tribe

just ask, 'What is it like to be Aboriginal?' I get a lot of questions from people on the streets in Redfern – they ask, 'Are you Aboriginal? What mob are you from?' Sometimes my mum walks away but I don't mind them asking.

When I finish school I want to go to university to be a vet or maybe a teacher. We want more Aboriginal teachers to teach us our culture.

If you don't know much about Aboriginal culture, just come and ask us. And please don't call us names.

About the author: Michelle McGrath

Born in Ireland, Michelle has called Australia home for more than 30 years and has always been especially interested in Aboriginal Australia. Michelle undertook tertiary studies and is a qualified Teacher's Assistant; she has followed her passion and has been working in the Indigenous Education Sector since 2018, currently being employed at Redfern Jarjum College, a special assistance school for Aboriginal and Torres Strait Islander children.

Growing up in Ireland amid a history of dispossession has made Michelle sympathetic to the Indigenous story. A story of land and culture ripped away, leaving behind a history of pain.

Michelle's passions lie in Indigenous education; both the education of our Indigenous children and the education of non-Indigenous children in Aboriginal culture and history.

To Michelle, it is very clear: young Aussies need to know the truth about what happened to Indigenous people when the white people came. Not so that blame can be laid, but so that they can understand the pain and how it has impacted the lives that so many Indigenous people are living today. Young Aussies need to learn about this history and they also need to learn about the rich culture of Indigenous Australia. This is a culture that needs to be nurtured and understood, and we all have a role to play.

About the artist: Garry Purchase

Garry is a proud Aboriginal man of Dharawal, Bidjigal descent. He grew up in Sydney's Eastern Suburbs in Botany and was raised within the Aboriginal community of La Perouse.

Garry has always had a creative passion and was a musician for many years, playing drums in a few Sydney rock bands. He started painting after he moved to the Central Coast with his wife and three sons in 2013. His style is a more modern take on traditional Aboriginal art, steering away from the common Dreamtime stories and focusing on his own personal journey, experiences and social issues. His work pushes a lot of creative boundaries as he stretches the limits of what Aboriginal art can be.

He has a very loyal fan base and has thousands of followers on social media. His works have attracted a lot of attention and have also earned him many awards. He took out the major first prize Tony Donovan Award at the Reconciliation Exhibition at Gosford Regional Gallery in both 2014 and 2016. Garry has been the recipient of the Aboriginal Health Award at the Mental

Health Art Works exhibition three times. At the time of writing, Garry is a finalist in the Gosford Art Prize.

Some of Garry's recent successes include a guest role on *Play School*, collaboration with homewares supplier Ladelle launching some really amazing products, collaboration with The Koori Curriculum as their artist in residence as well as supplying the artwork for their very successful books and marketing campaigns, and being the designer of an Indigenous range of balls for Footys4All.

Garry has recently been elected to the board of Bara Barang and hopes to make a positive contribution to the Central Coast community.

About the artist: Garry Purchase

Garry is a proud Aboriginal man of Dharawal, Bidjigal descent. He grew up in Sydney's Eastern Suburbs in Botany and was raised within the Aboriginal community of La Perouse.

Garry has always had a creative passion and was a musician for many years, playing drums in a few Sydney rock bands. He started painting after he moved to the Central Coast with his wife and three sons in 2013. His style is a more modern take on traditional Aboriginal art, steering away from the common Dreamtime stories and focusing on his own personal journey, experiences and social issues. His work pushes a lot of creative boundaries as he stretches the limits of what Aboriginal art can be.

He has a very loyal fan base and has thousands of followers on social media. His works have attracted a lot of attention and have also earned him many awards. He took out the major first prize Tony Donovan Award at the Reconciliation Exhibition at Gosford Regional Gallery in both 2014 and 2016. Garry has been the recipient of the Aboriginal Health Award at the Mental

Health Art Works exhibition three times. At the time of writing, Garry is a finalist in the Gosford Art Prize.

Some of Garry's recent successes include a guest role on *Play School*, collaboration with homewares supplier Ladelle launching some really amazing products, collaboration with The Koori Curriculum as their artist in residence as well as supplying the artwork for their very successful books and marketing campaigns, and being the designer of an Indigenous range of balls for Footys4All.

Garry has recently been elected to the board of Bara Barang and hopes to make a positive contribution to the Central Coast community.

Thanks

To the thirty contributors who opened their hearts to me when most of them didn't even know me! I thank you for sharing your stories and your truth. For many of you, revisiting these memories was a painful thing, and I would like to acknowledge your pain and thank you for sharing it so openly.

To Smart WFM, and its founder and CEO Jarrod McGrath, for supporting this book as part of their Pledge 1% philanthropy program. This book would not have been possible without their support.

I suffered from imposter syndrome throughout this whole writing process. I constantly questioned whether I was the right person to share these stories and whether anyone would appreciate them! These people gave me confidence and guidance when I needed it.

- Jarrod McGrath
- Raylene Carroll
- Andrew Griffiths
- Sandi Candotti
- Tina Brayan
- Marianne Rogan

And to all of my personal friends who continued to show interest and encourage me! My heartfelt thanks.

Thanks also go to the following people who shared their expertise with me during the process.

- Lesley Woodhouse
- Aziza Kuypers
- Dan Candotti, for the portraits of Mark and Ben
- Prof. Jakelin Troy
- Tess Denham Fabry
- John Ralph

And a special thanks to Julie Clarke Jones (also known as Julie Webb) and her family for granting me permission to use the word 'yellamundie' as the book's title.

www.ingramcontent.com/pod-product-compliance
Lightning Source LLC
Chambersburg PA
CBHW051331110526
44590CB00032B/4480